THE ONLINE TEACHING GUIDE

A Handbook of Attitudes, Strategies, and Techniques for the Virtual Classroom

Ken W. White
University of Phoenix Online Faculty

Bob H. Weight
University of Phoenix Online Faculty

Allyn and Bacon

Boston • London • Toronto • Sydney • Tokyo • Singapore

Executive Editor: Stephen D. Dragin
Series Editorial Assistant: Bridget McSweeney
Marketing Manager: Brad Parkins
Manufacturing Buyer: Dave Repetto

Library of Congress Cataloging-in-Publication Data

The online teaching guide : a handbook of attitudes, strategies, and
   techniques for the virtual classroom / Ken W. White, Bob H. Weight,
   editors
        p.   cm.
   Includes bibliographical references and index.
   ISBN 0-205-29531-2
   1. College teaching--Computer network resources.   2. Education,
Higher--Computer-assisted instruction.   I. White, Ken W.
II. Weight, Bob H.
LB1044.87.O45   1999
378.1'734--dc21   99-34779
                                                                   CIP

Printed in the United States of America

10 9 8 7 6 5 4   03 02 01

CONTENTS

PREFACE

The purpose of *The Online Teaching Guide: A Handbook of Attitudes, Strategies, and Techniques for the Virtual Classroom* is to respond to the questions posed by new online teachers, to place them at ease in their jobs, and to get them started effectively in the online classroom. The idea for the book comes from the growing need across the nation for teachers with the specific attitudes and skills for the online environment. In the past few years, the number of college and university courses offered to students via the Internet and the World Wide Web has increased exponentially. Numerous colleges and universities throughout the country are establishing distance learning programs, including online courses facilitated through computer-conferencing software.

Today, online is part of a new educational culture with its own distinct characteristics. Although not a panacea for educational change or reform, online education offers an important alternative. Like Zachary Karabell recognizes in his recent book, *What's College For? The Struggle to Define American Higher Education*, no one model, either traditional or online education, can possibly meet the needs of a system that encompasses 3,500 separate schools, millions of teachers, tens of millions of students, and billions of dollars. But online education does fill a niche in the changing nature of education in this country. Consequently, many traditional educators are either considering or making the transition to the online medium. Unfortunately, they do not always have the necessary skills to perform online teaching responsibilities effectively.

We researched aspects of this culture and the feasibility for this project partly by attending the Eighth Annual Meeting of the Western Cooperative for Educational Telecommunications in San Francisco in 1996. The Western Cooperative serves its members as a central clearinghouse for information and contacts; planner and facilitator of multistate projects; "spokesperson" to campus, state, and federal policy makers; provider of user support services; and evaluator and researcher on educational uses of telecommunications and information technologies. The theme of the conference was "Education in the Virtual Age" and we offered a preview of this book and asked the audience for feedback about the idea. The message was clear: The distance educators who attended the presentation expressed a strong interest. They saw the book as a much-needed training resource for the expanding opportunities in the field of electronically mediated learning.

The Online Teaching Guide is the result of the interest shown at that conference. The contributions were written by faculty members at the University of Phoenix Online Campus with over 100 years of collective teaching experience. The Online Campus, established in 1989, provides opportunities for working adult students whose schedules or geographical locations make it impractical to attend regularly scheduled classes. It offers a full-service learning environment in which students and instructors interact asynchronously using a computer conferencing system. It is designed to facilitate text-based individual and group discussions at any time, and from any place students and faculty happen to be.

This book contains ideas that have been developed, tested, and refined in hundreds of online classrooms at the University of Phoenix. The information provides countless learning opportunities for adult students struggling to improve their professional skills in the emerging information age and to play their educational roles with greater ease and success. The book is intended as a practical introduction for instructors, beginning or otherwise, who want useful ideas and techniques that will help them teach more effectively in the online classroom. It is not meant as a technical guide (we expect you to be able to turn on your computer and run your software), but as a valuable resource for conceptual issues and online instructional techniques.

While this guidebook offers practical tips on how to improve online communication and instructional skills, it also recognizes that there is much more to good online teaching than simply following tips. It assumes that its readers are thoughtful individuals who are committed to enhancing their online teaching and are capable of judging how the concepts and suggestions apply to their own situations.

In many ways, *The Online Teaching Guide* is a survival manual. It can help online teachers work their way through the recurring problems, challenges, and dilemmas they inevitably face in the virtual classroom. It can also help reduce the feelings of isolation that all teachers experience at some time or another—but particularly prevalent with online instructors—by offering a unique perspective about the online medium. Instead of focusing on approaches that see online teaching as simply the transmission of information—the correspondence course model, if you will—the book presents attitudes, strategies, and techniques that are *socially* based. Online education is not just an electronic medium where students buy their credits, do their work at home, study in isolation, and occasionally communicate with their instructor. It is an inherently relational and human process, not reducible to just sending and receiving electronic messages. The book's contributors show how the online medium is not only an irresistible mechanism for learning but it is also a way of relating to other human beings. The virtual university remains a social system consisting of interdependent people, events, and behaviors.

The social emphasis of *The Online Teaching Guide* is particularly poignant. Recently, a study from Carnegie Mellon University suggested users of the Internet become lonely and socially withdrawn. "The more people were online, the more signs they gave of being a little bit more socially isolated," said Robert Kraut, the lead author of the study (personnel correspondence, 1999). That is why *The Online Teaching Guide* suggests that online education requires a *value-added* approach. Teachers should use technology to enhance the complex private and social activities that make up the learning process. From this perspective, the online classroom exists to be evoked anytime, anywhere, by any learner, to facilitate social interaction and learning. Online education remains a social construct where learning—individual and social—is supported by computational technology, not the other way around.

Consequently, this book reflects a basic belief that effective online instruction requires an *interpersonal* approach. In contrast to the correspondence course model, online educators can overcome the sense of isolation often experienced by teachers and learners in the virtual world by expanding the definition of interpersonal communication to that world. Many people consider interpersonal communication to be limited to what can happen between two people—for example, husband and wife, parent and child, teacher and student—in primarily face-to-face situations. The writers in this book prefer to see it as a label for a type or *quality* of human interaction that can be present in a variety of situations, including the online classroom. Experience shows that online learning is always about dealing with people and that there are attitudes and behaviors that help online educators make "the interpersonal choice."

On the other hand, good teaching—online or otherwise—means more than relating with students. Beyond relational factors, good teaching requires practical classroom-management skills and a deep understanding of various instructional methods and techniques. It demands both meaningful reflection on the question of human relations and a systematic approach to the instructional process. The connections made by good teachers are not only held in the human engagement with students but also in the professional methods of instruction. Teaching is about student learning and deals with establishing conditions for facilitating learning. Although no single instructional practice or strategy is always superior to any other, good instructors must be at least aware of "best practices"—skills, abilities, and preferences—and be encouraged to adopt them.

Likewise, effective online education not only requires human contact; it demands instructional *structure* with aims, objectives, goals, and rhythms. Beginning as well as seasoned teachers must appreciate this prior to effective teaching. It is through structure—the manipulation of time and virtual space—that the online instructor shapes the social and content elements to inform and enhance the learning process. The teacher who has techniques that implement and facilitate structure—such as setting the tone, encouraging class participation, and getting the class organized—is more likely to get off to a good start and maintain it. Consequently, this book illustrates that the effective use of instructional technology requires specific characteristics that empower adult learners and encourage them to assume responsibilities for their own learning. It promotes characteristics such as the following:

- **Interaction and feedback.** Online students learn through active engagement with faculty and other students. Online learners need to know if their ideas and responses are productive.

- **Learner control.** With their busy schedules and work and family responsibilities, online students need to be able to stop at any time and to reenter at their convenience. *Synchronous learning,* where teachers and students communicate in "real time," offers a high degree of flexibility to many students; *asynchronous learning* offers more choice of where and, above all, when students access learning.
- **Directions and help.** Online learners require access to guidance. Instructors, other students, and software should prompt learners step by step through difficult information and activities.
- **Consistency and organization.** Explicit and consistent organization increases the retention of new material. Summaries, interaction, and feedback should organize and provide a synopsis of the material presented. Instructional segments should be short to accommodate "information overload" common in virtual situations. Online learners develop a sense of accomplishment when instruction is divided into modules, units, and subunits.
- **Assessment and record keeping.** A tracking system should inform online learners of the materials and activities they need to review before proceeding.

These points are supported and emphasized throughout this book. The purpose of Chapters 1 through 3 is to establish a firm foundation for readers to appreciate the importance of applying an interpersonal communication perspective to the online medium. Chapter 4 stresses the importance of learner control through the eyes of an online student. The importance of liberal arts to online education is discussed in Chapter 5. Chapters 6 through 10 offer specific and practical ways to incorporate consistency and organization into the online classroom through various forms of direction and help—facilitation, record keeping, and preparation. Chapter 11 and 12 return readers to the joys and sorrows of the online world by pointing to the fun of active learning and to the reality of virtual conflict. Then, it is back to some structural issues—teaching quantitative courses online and giving and getting useful online feedback—in Chapters 13 and 14. The organization of these chapters generally moves from macro issues about attitudes most needed by preservice or beginning online instructors to micro issues about specific strategies and techniques likely to be of more concern to the practicing online teacher.

Although this book is intended as a practical guidebook, it also shows how teaching shapes practice. In his 1990 book, *Scholarship Reconsidered* (Carnegie Foundation for the Advancement of Teaching), Ernest L. Boyer suggests a new way of defining scholarship that takes into account both theory and practice. Boyer argues that the work of educators might be thought of as having four separate, yet overlapping, professional functions: the scholarships of discovery, integration, application, and teaching. *Discovery* comes closest to what is meant by research; *integration* means interpreting data for meaning; *application* is engaging that meaning in practical ways; and *teaching* communicates meaning to others.

As you read through *The Online Teaching Guide,* you will find valuable scholarship, not necessarily in terms of original research, but in the three other ways. First, the text is designed to help you understand and walk yourself through the important landmarks and pathways of the online world. Written by experts in online education, each chapter is full of detailed information about course preparation, basic online teaching skills, techniques, tools, and methods. You will find redundancy, but we encourage you to accept this as intentional and noteworthy.

It is an indicator of *integration*. For example, the importance of tone is expressed throughout the book because a positive and supportive tone is a major pattern of effective online teaching.

Second, this is the first book to provide comprehensive guidance in the *application* of theory essential to successful online teaching. Although the authors share many themes, they also offer a variety of personal orientations. Each perspective is unique. This will help you reflect on both the breadth of online teaching issues and on the depth of the challenges that confront all online instructors.

Finally, this book is evidence of *scholarly teaching*. It is a dynamic learning tool containing the kinds of knowledge and techniques that lead to online teaching competence. New online teaching opportunities are appearing daily and we hope that *The Online Teaching Guide* will prepare you for a successful experience. We would appreciate hearing your comments regarding this book. You can e-mail us at:

Ken White   kenwwhite@email.uophx.edu

Bob Weight   bweight@lynx.csn.net

Acknowledgments

The Online Teaching Guide is truly an example of a collaborative effort. We thank the contributors who gave their time and efforts to a project offering little monetary reward. We appreciate that they are motivated by their love of teaching and by their continuing desire to make the University of Phoenix Online Campus and online education a good place and way to teach and learn. To the many colleagues at the Online Campus who freely shared their ideas and experiences, we offer our thanks. The contributors of this book represent a small percentage of the talent that exists at the Online Campus and, more than anything else, this book is an expression of that culture.

In this regard, we thank Karl Guaby, executive director of compliance at the University of Phoenix. His early advice helped us balance the needs of this project with the more general needs of the university. We found it a very creative and productive balance. A special thanks goes to Terri Bishop, former vice president of distance learning at the University of Phoenix; Anita Bischoff, former director of academic affairs at the Online Campus; and Bill Pepicello, associate vice president for academic affairs for the University of Phoenix for helping us maintain the balance.

Ken thanks colleagues at Everett Community College for their moral and technical support: Dale Hensley, dean of social science; Anita Newman, instructional technician; and Cathy Groger, secretary for faculty support. He also thanks his friend, Chad Lewis, for his always-helpful advice and assistance on difficult manuscripts.

Ken feels special gratitude for his wife, Liz, for making it possible for him to find the time to perform editing duties and for keeping things sane in the meantime. This book is mainly the brainchild of Bob, but Ken brought his writing and editing skills as well as a significant time commitment to the project. By helping with the revision of manuscripts and by picking up the domestic slack, Liz gave Ken the time he needed and she gave their sons, Nathan and Jamie, the attention they deserve.

We also thank the students at the University of Phoenix Online Campus and the people at Allyn and Bacon, particularly Steve Dragin, for making this book happen at all.

Finally, we sadly acknowledge the recent loss of Jim Farrar, University of Phoenix online faculty member, contributor to this book, and friend. Jim passed away in April 1999, and we shall all miss him. He touched our lives and made the online environment a more human place to teach.

ABOUT THE AUTHORS
AND CONTRIBUTORS

Authors

Ken White holds a M.Ed. from Western Washington University and an M.A. and a Ph.D. in speech communications from the University of Washington. He is a faculty member at Everett Community College in Washington state, where he teaches education and speech classes and has received The Outstanding Faculty of the Year Award. His interests include organizational, interpersonal, and instructional communication, and his experience includes assisting the College of Arts and Sciences at the University of Washington in developing and initiating a nationally recognized training program to improve the performance of undergraduate faculty and teaching assistants. Ken has written a number of journal articles, and his text, co-authored with Elwood N. Chapman, *Organizational Communication: An Introduction to Communication and Human Relation Strategies* (Simon and Schuster Custom Publishing), is used by the University of Phoenix. He has taught online courses for UOP for over six years in the areas of general education, organizational communication and behavior, and ethics. He recently completed his term as assistant department chair for general studies at the Online Campus, San Francisco, and as a member of the university's academic cabinet. E-mail: Kenwwhite@email.uophx.edu or white_kenw@msn.com

Bob Weight received his bachelor's degree in 1962 from the United States Air Force Academy, and his master's degree in aeronautical engineering in 1963 from the University of Michigan. After flight testing aircraft at Edwards Air Force Base and Wright-Patterson Air Force Base, he joined United Airlines in San Francisco. During his career with United, he served as a strategic planner, maintenance services manager, and manager of reservations sales and ticketing. After serving as vice president of operations at Rocky Mountain Airways, and director of maintenance at Frontier, he entered the public sector and now serves as the fleet manager for the city of Lakewood, Colorado. Bob has taught at the University of Phoenix since 1982 and has served as the senior faculty member of the Colorado Campus, area chair for General Management, and on many university-wide faculty committees dealing with academic issues. He has authored several courses in the strategic planning area. He was one of the first Online Campus faculty members and has been active in the development of the computer as an educational medium. He has received several awards from students, administration, and colleagues for his teaching abilities and commitment to the University of Phoenix. E-mail: bweight@lynx.csn.net

Contributors

Patricia Addesso is a consultant, teacher, public speaker, and author. She has worked for over 20 years in retail, academic, and telecommunications organizations, and has a doctorate in industrial/organizational psychology. She is currently head of PJA Consulting and specializes in organization development and team building. She is adjunct staff at the Center for Creative Leadership in San Diego, where she provides intensive one-on-one feedback and coaching to executives. Patricia teaches at the San Diego and Online Campuses at the University of Phoenix, where she specializes in management, strategic planning, and organizational Behavior courses. She also teaches management classes at San Diego State University's American Language Institute—a summer program for international executives—and at the United States International University. She is the author of *Management Would be Easy...If It Weren't for the People* (1996, AMACOM—The American Management Association). E-mail: Paddesso@aol.com

Al Badger spent the first 18 years of his life in Massachusetts and did most of his undergraduate work at the University of Massachusetts, where he received a B.A. in Chinese. He began teaching in Tunghai University, Taiwan, where he learned to read, write, and speak Mandarin Chinese. After three years of teaching, he became a student at the Ohio State University, where he earned a master's degree in education, focusing on English-as-a-second-language curriculum development. Al is currently the director of student services at the University of Phoenix Online Campus and provides educational advice as a teacher-pager for AOL, where he also submits a cartoon strip called "Phritzy's World." He has been studying and teaching T'ai Ch'i Chuan, a form of martial art and meditation, for over 23 years and is happy to teach anyone how to relax. E-mail: ajbadger@dnai.com

Anita Bischoff served as the director of academic affairs for the University of Phoenix Online Campus from 1995, when she completed the coursework for a doctorate in higher education administration at the University of California at Berkeley, to 1999. She holds two master's degrees, one in counseling and the other in higher education administration. She has supervised the recruiting and training of hundreds of faculty members as well as online curriculum and faculty governance. Anita gives many presentations at national conferences on the topic of online education. In past years, she taught English in Tokyo, served as a student union director for Nebraska Wesleyan University, and held numerous student services positions at St. Cloud State University in Minnesota. She has studied in England (while living in a castle) for her second undergraduate school year. She hails from Hibbing, Minnesota. E-mail: abischoff@earthlink.net

Terri Bishop was vice president of Distance Learning at the University of Phoenix for the Apollo Group. Since 1982, she has worked in a variety of capacities for Apollo, the educational company that oversees the management of the Institute for Professional Development, Western International University, the College of Financial Planning, and the University of Phoenix. Terri has served in the areas of institutional licensure and accreditation, curriculum and technology development, and academic outcome assessment. She was responsible for the initial development, implementation, and growth of the University of Phoenix Online Campus. E-mail: terribishop@mindspring.com

Jim Farrar was a consultant to business on Total Quality Assurance and ISO-9000 International Quality Standards. He was a voting member of the United States Advisory Group to International Standards Organization/Technical Committee 69 on Statistical Methods and an active member of the ISO 9000 International Forum. In 1992, he was invited as a delegate with the Small Business and Management delegation to the Citizen's Ambassador Program in Russia, Latvia, and Estonia. He has held engineering and management positions with aerospace companies such as TRW, Collins Radio Company, Ford Aerospace, and Motorola Inc. Jim joined the University of Phoenix in 1981, teaching finance, statistics, and business research. He joined the Online Campus in 1991 and held the position of instructional specialist from 1996 to 1999. He also served as the Area Chair for Finance, Assistant Department Chair for Graduate Programs, and received the Distinguished Faculty Award for the Online Campus 1993. He earned his B.S. from the University of New Mexico and an M.B.A. from Pepperdine School of Business and Management. Jim was completing his D.B.A. (ABD) from Nova Southeastern University.

Marilyn Fullmer-Umari is a management consultant and trainer in the areas of organizational development and human resource management. She has two master's degrees in management and human resource management from Cornell University. She is also a faculty member at the University of Phoenix, where she teaches graduate and undergraduate classes in organizational behavior, culture, and human resource management. E-mail: hrsa@ix.netcom.com

Arlene Hiss grew up in the little town of Derby, Connecticut, where her family still lives. She attended High Point University in High Point, North Carolina, receiving her bachelor's degree in physical education. The next 16 years were spent teaching high school dance and physical education. Her M.B.A. is from Azusa Pacific University in Azusa, California, and her Ph.D. in leadership and human behavior is from United States International University in San Diego. Arlene has taught high school, worked for General Motors, and was a race car driver from 1962 until 1976, where she was the first woman to race an Indianapolis car in the Phoenix 150 and the first woman to race a late-model stock car in the Texas 500. She has her own consulting group in education and employee development specializing in train-the-trainer. She joined the University of Phoenix in April of 1991 and was honored with the Online Campus Distinguished Faculty of the Year Award at the 1995 graduation. E-mail: alhiss@email.uophx.edu

Chad Lewis has served as an online faculty member for the University of Phoenix since 1990 and has been on the business faculty of Everett Community College since 1979. He has coauthored microcomputer simulations and textbooks distributed by U.S. publishers covering the topics of general business, marketing, and management. He has also published extensively in academic and trade journals on the subjects of marketing, decision making, conflict, leadership, compensation, and educational technology. Chad earned a B.A. from the Evergreen State College, an M.Ed. from Western Washington University, and an M.B.A. from the University of Puget Sound. He is listed in *Who's Who Among America's Teachers* (1996), *Who's Who in the World* (1995), *Who's Who in Emerging Leaders in the United States* (1991), *Who's Who in American Education* (1991), and *Who's Who in the West* (1989). E-mail: chadlewis@email.uophx.edu

Bill Pepicello is associate vice president for academic affairs at the University of Phoenix. He was born and raised in Pennsylvania and went to graduate school at Brown University, where he earned a master's and doctorate in linguistics. He has taught English, psychology, and anthropology at the University of Delaware and at Temple University, where he was also chairman of the Classics Department. Bill moved to the West Coast in 1985. After a brief stint at University of the Pacific, he became a teacher and administrator with National University. He joined the University of Phoenix in 1995 as the dean of General Studies. He has written a book and several articles on humor, specializing in how children develop a sense of humor. E-mail: wjpepice@email.uophx.edu

Shelia Porter was awarded a Juris Doctor degree from the University of Colorado in 1984 and began a civil litigation practice that same year. In 1997, she coauthored the Porter Jackson Mediation Style Indicator and wrote a chapter on Alternative Dispute Resolution (ADR) for the *Annual Survey of Colorado Law*. Before attending law school, she graduated summa cum laude and Phi Beta Kappa from Kent State University in Ohio with a major in Spanish and a minor in secondary education. Later, she held a graduate teaching fellowship and enjoyed working with adult learners. Shelia's current professional passion comes from her mediation practice and teaching. She joined the faculty of the Colorado Campus of the University of Phoenix in 1991 and the Online Campus in 1993. She has developed mediation and business conflict management courses for onsite classes at the University of Phoenix and has adapted business law courses and an Intellectual Property Management course for the Online Campus. She currently combines her communication, problem-solving, teaching, and computer skills in her work as an instructional specialist for the Online Campus of the University of Phoenix. E-mail: sdporter@email.uophx.edu

Lorraine Priest lives in Shelby Township, Michigan. She currently works for General Motors' Service Technology Group. For 22 years at General Motors, she has been a supervisor, a reliability engineer, troubleshooter, trainer, installer of plant floor systems and mainframe communications, a cost accountant, and implementation manager for the new Warranty Reporting System. She is dedicated to her husband and their two cats, to Northern Michigan, and to resting in their log cabin in Atlanta, Michigan, where deer, elk, and turkeys feed in the yard. Lorraine is a graduate of the University of Phoenix and was selected as the graduation speaker for both her undergraduate and graduate classes. Her goal is to complete her doctorate studies.

Fred Schwartz is the assistant department chair for business and management at the University of Phoenix Online Campus. He is also a principal consultant at Business Solutions Unlimited, a management and computer systems technology integration consulting firm in Manhattan Beach, California. He spent 21 years in various management roles in the aerospace and defense industries and 10 years with Walt Disney Imagineering, where he managed project planning and scheduling, and designed and presented management-training courses in project management techniques. During nine years with the University of Phoenix, Fred has held various faculty governance positions and developed curriculum for numerous online and onsite courses. He presently facilitates courses in management, technology, and project management at the Online Campus. He earned his B.S. from the University of Cincinnati and his M.B.A. from Pepperdine University. E-mail: fritz123@email.uophx.edu

Marilyn Simon received her B.A. from the City University of New York at Brooklyn College in mathematics education, her M.S. from the Illinois Institute of Technology in Chicago in applied mathematics, and her Ph.D. from Walden University in Minneapolis in mathematics, education, and technology. She also did postdoctorate research at the Institute of Advanced Studies at Princeton on women in mathematics. She has been actively involved in mathematics and computer science education since 1969 and has taught all areas of mathematics from preschool through graduate school. Marilyn is president of Best-Prep, LLC, and Math Power, international educational consulting firms. Her publications include *The Dissertation Cookbook, I Can Do Math, Math Mastery, Math Advantage, Math Start, Mountains Are Not Triangles: A Maiden Voyage through Chaos Theory and Fractal Geometry,* and *Math Advancement.* E-mail: mksimon@email.uophx.edu

Elizabeth Tice has 15 years of experience in higher education in administration, counseling, and instruction. She is a trained Gestalt Therapist and is currently on the Board of Directors for the Southwestern Gestalt Foundation. She is also currently the dean of the School of General Studies at the University of Phoenix. Prior to that, she was the director of the UOP Assessment Program. Liz has published articles in the *CAEL News and Forum, The Adult Learning Journal,* and the *Journal of Excellence in Higher Education.* She is currently pursuing a Ph.D. in human science at Saybrook Graduate School. E-mail: ettice@apollogrp.edu

1

FACE TO FACE IN
THE ONLINE CLASSROOM
Keeping It Interpersonal and Human

KEN WHITE

Effective online instruction requires both content knowledge and interpersonal skills because the challenges of the online instructor are essentially about human interaction. Although the online environment depends on computer-mediated communication, it involves people in ways that other examples of distance education may not. Unlike technological forms of the correspondence course or interactive television programs, online education is structured around the dynamics of human communication and it features the traditional equivalents of due dates, study groups, and class discussions. Although it is an electronic medium for transmitting content, it is also a human arena for the exchange of ideas. As in any social venture, people are imprecise, unclear, and unpredictable. But most importantly, because of its special circumstances, it is even more challenging to work through the uncertainties and ambiguities of online communication.

Online teaching depends on effective communication attitudes and behaviors. Many of the frustrations that beginning online instructors experience are directly related to how they perceive—often subconsciously—communication and its relationship to their students. Limited perceptions often direct ineffective online communication behaviors. For example, the online medium at the University of Phoenix is completely textual. There is the likely assumption that meaning is primarily in the words on the computer screen. If communication with online students is seen as only a matter of precision or correct grammar, the online classroom becomes a narrow and frustrating place to work through the inherent complexities of all human communication.

Beginning online instructors should be especially prepared to cope with the ambiguities of computer-mediated communication. They must develop the understanding that meaning is created in the interaction among people—not in the words alone—and that online communication is more than electronic verbal images. It includes all the human qualities of attitudes, feelings, and emotions.

This chapter suggests that the preparation of new online instructors should begin with the awareness of how they can choose to be interpersonal in the online classroom. This includes an understanding of how choice is always a part of human communication, particularly in the online classroom. This point is critical: Over a decade of experience as a communication instructor has shown me that people believe that circumstances, situations, and other individuals often force them to communicate one way or another. It is common for people to think they have limited or no choices when it comes to certain communication circumstances, even though they always have the choice to react negatively or respond thoughtfully to things that happen to them and to what other people say and do.

Choice plays a key role in online communication and teaching. It is my hope in this chapter that by looking at the role of choice in communication, and by redefining the concept of interpersonal communication, beginning online instructors will be empowered to influence their future communication encounters in the electronic classroom in a positive way.

Mutating Communication Metaphors

Developing effective choices in online communication starts with looking at how people perceive communication. For example, people who see communication as *debate* may limit their choices in such a way as to encourage negative arguments, or what onliners call *flaming*. If people feel they are in a debate, they naturally try to argue and win. Communication does not have to be seen as a debate, however. In contrast, some people see communication in other ways—for example, as a conversation. They appreciate that by seeing communication as a conversation, people put their choices into a broader perspective. If people do not have to win, they are less inclined to argue or flame.

Organizational theorist Karl Weick describes how people's communication behavior is based on guiding metaphors. He uses the phrase *mutate your metaphors* to describe the skill of changing how one views communication. In Weick's sense, *mutate* means change and *metaphor* means the major images people carry around in their hearts and minds to describe communication.

As Weick (1969) points out, guiding metaphors may not be at the conscious level and effort is required to bring them to awareness. To illustrate this, I do an onsite classroom activity where I draw a chalk line on the board that represents what individuals typically identify as a bird or seagull. I then ask the class, "What do you see?" Students immediately respond, "Bird!" "Seagull!" I then ask again, "What do you see?" For a moment, students look confused, but then a hearty soul joins the game and hollers, "Mountains!" Another yells, "A sideways number three!" "Eyebrows!" The responses mount until they sometimes reach 15 or 20. (I always know when the students are fully in the game and actively playing with mutating their metaphors. It is at that point that someone screams out a part of the human anatomy.)

This awareness activity shows that people do not always consciously know when they see things one way or another, but they can change their metaphors and perceptions if they are encouraged to try. Awareness and change are important because the misuse of metaphors often leads to personal and professional problems, including in the online teaching environment.

People communicate in the online classroom based on their guiding metaphors, and it is important that people analyze those metaphors and their possible consequences. Metaphors can be deeply flawed. If a metaphor represents a narrow, shallow view of communication or a situation, it can lead to the inability to articulate a careful analysis of problems and to the alienation of people. Again, seeing communication as something like war distorts and limits thoughtful responses. If you expect a war, for instance you line up all of your communication "weapons" and "attack your opponent." You are definitely not in the state of mind to be open to what the other person has to say or to let down your defenses and disclose some personal information. Common sports metaphors, along with other outmoded images such as the military and cowboys, can become obsessive. People and organizations lose the capacity to think and act appropriately because they are trapped subconsciously in an irrelevant and inappropriate system of thought and communication.

As conceptual frameworks in the online classroom, metaphors are either helpful or rooted in an irrelevant past. Online students can be seen either as human beings who use technology to construct their own knowledge and meaning, or as empty vessels on the other end of the computer that need to be filled with data. When metaphors are useful, they clarify complex teaching and learning situations by drawing on simpler and less ambiguous images of life. The way a person talks and writes shapes the way that person looks at the world, the way he or she thinks, and the way he or she teaches.

As Weick observes, a person needs to consciously choose when it is useful to see communication in a different way. Online instructors must mutate their metaphors about communication's specific form in the online classroom and begin seeing interpersonal communication in ways more appropriate to the situation. The next section will discuss an approach for accomplishing this.

Online Interpersonal Communication

One way that online instructors can mutate their metaphors and increase their sense of choice about online communication is by redefining the concept of *interpersonal communication*. As a metaphor for choosing how to interact with people, interpersonal communication is often considered to be limited to what happens between two people—such as husband and wife, parent and child, employer and employee, teacher and student—in mostly primarily face-to-face situations. But this perspective is only one way of seeing interpersonal communication. *Interpersonal* can also be defined as a type or *quality* of communication that can be present in a variety of situations. As a quality, interpersonal communication happens in a variety of settings—on the phone, through writing, in committees or other groups, and even on the computer.

Because the online environment is so technologically dependent, there is a particular need for instructors to mutate their interpersonal metaphor and to think about the quality of online communication. John Stewart, professor, mentor, and friend, offers a way with his *Interpersonal–Impersonal Continuum*. This visual tool or metaphor points to the many possibilities for interpersonal communication in the online classroom. It emphasizes that interpersonal communication is not restricted to situations such as the number of people or face-to-face contact, but is a result of the choice one makes in the online environment.

Imagine the continuum:

INTERPERSONAL - **IMPERSONAL**

The continuum functions by emphasizing that one may choose to place a communication situation anywhere on the quality spectrum. It is no longer a question of *either* impersonal *or* interpersonal communication, but of degrees. For example, a person may choose to put an online class-room on the interpersonal end of the continuum. The individual moves specific situations left or right along the continuum depending on his or her choice to be more or less interpersonal. No matter what the situation, the Interpersonal–Impersonal Continuum assumes that a person has a choice to be more or less interpersonal.

But on what does the choice depend? How does an individual know if he or she should choose to make his or her online communication more or less interpersonal? What are the specific qualities at each end of the continuum? Stewart (1990) suggests that there are three reasons for making the choice to be more or less interpersonal in communication situations, all recognizing that communication is dealing with people.

First, one chooses to be more interpersonal in order to focus on what makes the other person unique. An object can be the same as any other object. For example, if I want to put new batteries in my shortwave radio so that I can listen to the BBC, any AA batteries will work. In a similar vein, any brand computer disk can be properly formatted to work in the computer that I used to write this chapter.

Online students are never interchangeable, even though they might seem so if their instructor allows them to become only letters on a computer screen. As Sproull and Kiesler (1991) observe, computer-based communication creates new social situations. Reminders of other people and conventions for communicating are weak. This *deindividuation* occurs in the online environment because students have anonymity and lack social reminders. In the online class, messages are likely to show less social awareness, politeness, and concern for other's individuality. It is easy to understand, then, why online students can treat each other and can be treated by their instructors so impersonally. This practice is never appropriate, however. They are as different from each other as people in any other social situation. They differ in personal styles and tastes, religious preferences, and political views. Although the electronic medium of the online classroom may reduce social awareness, online instructors must move beyond the medium and create opportunities for students to share their unique experiences and traits.

Online instructors can recognize that their students are unique by carefully designing courses, instructional materials, and activities that communicate to students that learning fits personal and unique characteristics and skills. Too frequently, instructors do not consider the impact of course design on student learning. Courses are often designed from a technical and efficiency perspective and little attention is given to how the course fits the person. For example, my online students must pose questions as part of their coursework. Student-initiated questions add life to a course and students enjoy struggling with issues in which they have a stake or interest.

Second, one chooses to be more interpersonal in order to show respect for a person's ability to think and make choices. Objects do not think like humans do. That is because objects can only be chosen; they cannot choose. Human beings are capable of making choices and initiating action. A computer can seem to operate on its own, but it continues to be dependent on choices initiated from the outside. (This second point needs elaboration. Often, people who are physically challenged are treated like objects because they do not appear capable of initiating actions. But there is a difference between the movements of objects and the actions of people. While movements are fundamentally reflexive in nature, actions are reflective. Even though people can be limited in movement, they are still capable of initiating actions. People are reflective. So the issue is not whether the physically challenged are able to act, but what the means are to communicate those thoughts and actions.)

Nowhere is thinking more evident than in the textual environment of the online classroom. If writing is thinking, then online students display their thinking throughout the course, illustrating their individual styles and changing attitudes. Online instructors can show recognition for their students' thinking by maintaining high standards of rigor that challenge students and by building opportunities for choice into their online courses. For example, in my own online classes, I am open to student suggestions about changes in the course, either the present course or future courses. As Chapter 14 will show, I seek out my students' thoughts and will often change the content, rhythm, or activities of a course in order to respond to their choices.

Online instructors must recognize that their students are thinkers and give them tasks that are complex enough to be challenging but simple enough to accomplish. If an assignment is too complex, it is frustrating and not satisfying. If it is too simple, it is boring. Consequently, successfully challenging an online student requires a high level of open communication and feedback between online teachers and students.

Third, one chooses to be more interpersonal in order to pay attention to relevant feelings and to the whole human being. Humans have feelings. This quality is what distinguishes humans from objects more than anything else does. Stewart (1990) offers this example: If you kick a rock, you could probably predict what would happen. If you had information on such things as force, velocity, momentum, and energy, you might even be able to predict exactly where the rock would end up after you kicked it. But try kicking a person. What will be the human reaction? Will the person cry, look surprised, get angry, or kick you back? You take your chances with the human factor because emotions and feelings cannot be measured and calculated. Sure, a person's brain waves, heart rate, pulse, and respiration are measured, but that's not the whole person. How people react emotionally to the experiences of their lives and to events continues to be immeasurable.

Likewise, the online classroom is an emotional environment. As many contributors point out in the following chapters, and as I emphasize in Chapter 12, online messages are often startlingly blunt and can escalate into flaming. In the face of these uncertainties, online instructors must adopt attitudes and strategies to remind themselves and their students that they are social actors in an emotional situation. For example, one theme throughout this book is that online instructors can add typographical cues, or *emoticons,* to their messages to signal attitude and mood.

Online instructors can help develop the whole student by establishing a positive and supportive overall emotional climate through such techniques as emoticons, effective conflict management, and constructive feedback. (All these topics will be covered later in this book.) A positive emotional climate can serve as a frame of reference for online student activities and will therefore shape individual expectancies, attitudes, feelings, and behaviors throughout a program.

There are occasions when communication needs to be more efficient and impersonal. In those cases, one chooses to (1) focus on the general characteristics of people, (2) ignore the issue of thinking and choice, and (3) stay away from wholeness and emotions. For example, when I am talking with a bank teller, a situation where just the two of us are in a face-to-face encounter (normally what one would think of as an interpersonal situation), the continuum opens up the possibility that communication can still be on the impersonal end of the scale. Neither the bank teller nor I want to hold up a long line while we have a personal chat and recognize each other's uniqueness, feelings, and choice. When two people are in a face-to-face situation, that does not necessarily mean that communication is or should be interpersonal. Neither interpersonal nor impersonal communication is always inappropriate. Because of expectations, time constraints, or a multitude of other factors, the impersonal approach is sometimes the only way to deal efficiently with a situation.

But online instructors must keep in mind that their situation is a different one. Two features of the online classroom combine to make it a relatively unstructured communication situation. First, it relies entirely on plain text for sending messages. Second, the plain text is temporary, appearing and disappearing from the screen. These two features make it easy for both online instructors and students to forget or ignore the person on the other end of the computer. There are no strict rules or formulas for making communication decisions in any situation—only guidelines that help people make particular choices as communicators. But it is crucially important in the online world to remember that people always have choices. They may choose to be interpersonal in such unexpected settings as teaching over a computer.

Person Building and Educating Online Students

Another of Stewart's (1990) concepts can sum up the preceding ideas—person building. *Person building* is the idea that the quality of each person's life is a result of the quality of the communication he or she experiences. In other words, *person building is a consequence of interpersonal communication.* Communication can be a tool to accomplish certain instructional tasks, but it also is a process that affects who students are as people. As any schoolteacher knows, there is a big difference between what a teacher says to a student (the tool part) and how a teacher says it (the person-building part). Teachers can tell a student, "You're wrong," and emphasize being correct, or they can ask, "What's another way of getting the answer," and emphasize problem solving.

Online educators, like other educators, are fundamentally in the business of person building. As in all classrooms, person building is the foundation for learning and growth in the online classroom. It is the quality of human contact that continually develops online students—constantly reforming who they are and who they will become. Whenever the instructor communicates interpersonally online, he or she participates in the building of people and shares in their learning and growth.

Other questions arise at this point: Where is this leading? What kind of people does the teacher want his or her online students to become? It is important that online students are treated as unique, thinking, and emotional individuals, and that we, as educators, participate in their growth. But what is the ultimate goal?

As a means for responding to these questions, I look to Virginia Voeks of San Diego University. As an experiment, Voeks (1979) asked people she knew, who had gone to college or a university, what they studied and what kinds of jobs they got. Voeks was surprised at the variety of jobs each person had held and the apparent unrelatedness of the person's major to his or her subsequent occupations. Voeks questioned whether this meant that college is unimportant. To the contrary, Voeks determined that college is even more important, for it prepares students for a large range of occupations and for a widening way of living.

Likewise, if online education is seen as more than the electronic transmission of bits of information—if it is a human arena for interpersonal contact and person building—then it too should be preparing students for a satisfying life. Online education is a tool to accomplish certain vocational tasks, but it is also a process that affects who students are as people. Voeks (1979) suggests some general goals that heighten the chances of a student becoming "a highly educated person" and that can be readily applied to the online environment:

- *Online students should learn to comprehend this world and go on learning.* It is important that students understand that a fund of information and ideas is a set of tools. Students will be able to solve more problems reasonably and interpret more events. However, if students are taught only to collect and store facts, they will become little more than databanks. The mere possession of information is worthless. Online educators can begin the journey of educating online students by recognizing that information does not constitute being "educated." That's why the University of Phoenix stresses faculty members as practitioners. To be educated, online students must develop other attributes.
- *Online students should learn to see relationships and make more meaningful integrations.* *Integration* refers to the synthesis of materials and a tying together of concepts, information, and ideas. With integration skills, the online student can make each new fact more meaningful and comprehensible. For example, an understanding of organizational behavior or management can be enhanced through the reading of literature. Instead of just the facts, students can confront issues about the quality of life in materials such as the book *The Jungle* or the video *Wallstreet.*
- *Online students should be exposed to deeper and widening interests.* As Chapter 5 of this book will argue, the liberal arts and general studies have an important role to play in online education. They expose students to deeper interests and other ways of living. Online students should be given the chance to share in other students' lives and to gain appreciation for individual differences. College should furnish many opportunities for perceiving the value of difference and for learning to act in accord with these perceptions. For example, controversy should be encouraged in the online classroom though managed carefully. If done properly, teaching through controversy reveals a difference of opinion while promoting tolerance for diversity. Techniques such as "cooperative controversy" (Bredehoft, 1991) can help the online classroom become a laboratory in which beneficial group

learning takes place through controversial issues. When questions such as "Should new laws be enacted to limit foreign countries from buying U.S. property?" or "Are art exhibits such as photographs by Robert Mapplethorpe pornographic, and should they be supported by taxpayers' money?" are addressed through careful procedures like cooperative controversy, online students can learn new ways of thinking.

Thus, the person-building metaphor highlights the central importance of interpersonal communication and a broad education in the online environment. It suggests that online instructors can communicate in such a way as to play a role in helping students learn information and develop as people. Online education is not just about the transmission of information. It depends on a friendly, relaxed, and congenial classroom with a teacher who shows respect for students, who is concerned about their needs, and who is supportive. In other words, online education—as a process of training and developing the knowledge, skills, minds, and characters of learners—arises from and is sustained by broader instructional goals and practices. Although technological factors strongly influence the online learning climate, their effects must be mediated by the human interaction facilitated by the online instructor. It is the quality of relationships that is crucial. No contact is more central to the education of an online student than the human one.

Conclusion

The way day-to-day teaching functions in the online environment is, in part, a result of how teachers perceive communication and its relationship to the human factor. Choice making is a necessary part of online communication and offers a way for responding to various instructional challenges and situations, but appropriate choices depend on the ability to see communication situations in a variety of ways. Likewise, changing the guiding metaphors used for clarifying complex communication situations helps reveal online communication choices. What might have been considered an impersonal setting is reframed to have many interpersonal possibilities. An interaction with an online student becomes an opportunity to affect the quality of that student's life.

Overall, this chapter has reinforced the idea that effective online teaching is twofold: the ability to transmit messages clearly and accurately, and the ability to maintain positive interpersonal relationships. In fact, the chapter has tried to tilt the balance between these two functions in the online environment a little more to the interpersonal side. In many ways, it suggests that, to paraphrase the German philosopher Karl Jaspers, the online instructor's supreme achievement in the virtual world is communication from personality to personality.

That said, I will leave you with a few reminders for improving online interpersonal communication and teaching skills:

- *Watch your communication metaphors.* Effectiveness in today's online learning environments begins with a broader, more realistic picture of the people and the communication that makes up virtual organizations.
- *Treat your online students as unique.* Use your students' names in all correspondence and have online students upload a brief biography at the beginning of each class. Encourage them to share their life stories as well as ideas about the course. Do not ignore the fact that even a simple thing like a message sent to a student's personal mailbox where you ask how things are going helps to build self-esteem and a positive sense of individuality.
- *Build choice into your online courses and teaching behaviors.* People make choices about how to communicate in the online classroom based on past choices, perceptions of the current situation, and the ability to see communication situations differently. Assume that you have choices when it comes to online teaching and look for possibilities. Choose to be interpersonal. Look for opportunities to treat online students as thinking human beings. Practice open communication while setting high standards.
- *Actively contribute to a positive emotional climate.* As often as possible, use interpersonal communication to encourage online interaction and to build collective trust. Manage online conflict and practice constructive feedback. In addition, as Chapter 3 will stress, use humor. Humor is a useful online perspective of looking at and coping with electronic technology and human interaction.

And finally, remember, more than anything else, effective online education is about more than merely sending messages or accomplishing instructional tasks—it is about building educated people.

References

Bredehoft, D. J. (1991). Cooperative controversies in the classroom. *College Teaching, 39* (3), 122–125.

Sproull, L., & Kiesler, S. (1991*). Connections: New Ways of Working in the Networked Organization.* Cambridge, MA: The MIT Press.

Stewart, J. (1990). *Bridges Not Walls.* New York: McGraw-Hill.

Voeks, V. (1979). *On Becoming an Educated Person.* Philadelphia: W. B. Saunders.

Weick, K. (1969). *The Social Psychology of Organizing.* Reading, MA: Addison-Wesley.

2

TAMING THE LIONS AND TIGERS AND BEARS

The WRITE WAY to Communicate Online

CHAD LEWIS

Dorothy and her pals didn't have a choice on their journey to Oz. They had to make it to the Emerald City. Online instructors and students are in the same fix in the sense that, once committed to the virtual classroom, there is no way to avoid communicating online. And, for many, the virtual classroom holds the lions and tigers and bears of the story.

The primary purpose of this chapter is to help instructors tame the beasts—first by contributing to the understanding of the dynamics underlying online communication and then by offering perspectives, a framework, and rules for improving it.

Communication Complexities: "We're Not in Kansas Anymore!"

Before delving into nuances of online communication, it is important first to discuss complexities of good old-fashioned, face-to-face communication—the sort of communication people engage in everyday. As Chapter 1 suggested, interpersonal communication is inherently complex. It is fraught with the potential for misunderstanding, even without the added burden of communicating through a modem.

Take, for example, the fuzzy nature of language. The words that are communicated may be understandable. However, the *why* of communication may be less so. For example, you may interpret my comment, "I like fish," to mean I enjoy broiled salmon steak with lemon juice and tartar sauce when, in fact, I was really trying to communicate a special fondness for a pet goldfish named Sherbet. Words can be as slippery as goldfish.

Besides the fuzziness of language, miscommunication also occurs because of invalid *attributions*. Human begins are "sense-making" creatures. We can form very clear attributions of others from just a small sample of communication and other information. We continually filter observations selectively, subject to recency and order effects, form a prototype based on those observations, and fill in the gaps of the prototype where necessary, oftentimes erroneously (Feldman, 1981).

Here is an example. Take a second and make your choices:

Mary is healthy, wealthy, and (smart, stupid).
Larry is bright, lively, and (fat, slender).

Most of you decided that Mary is smart and Larry is slender. Of course, wealthy people can be stupid, and bright people can be fat. However, most Americans have been socialized to make the associations of "smart" and "slender," respectively, in this exercise. Of course, prototype formation concerning characteristics of Mary and Larry will become more accurate as more information about these people becomes available.

Attributions are also profoundly influenced by a person's frame of reference. Two people can receive the same communication and, as a function of coming from very different backgrounds, can reach two very different conclusions about the meaning of a particular communication.

Sometimes, the difference is simply perceptual. Independent of frame of reference, one person sees or hears something different from what another sees or hears, even when both parties are part of the same communication. In April 1997, a Boston disc jockey at WZLX-FM mentioned an incredible set of connections between the Pink Floyd album, *Dark Side of the Moon,* and the film, *The Wizard of Oz.* The claim is that the album music and events on the screen coincide. (To see the magic, you have to start the album at the third roar of the MGM lion and, of course, you have to watch *The Wizard of Oz* with the sound turned off.) Are the connections real? Not according to members of the band, Pink Floyd. Kennedy (1997) offers one explanation: "While it is true, as anyone who's watched MTV with the sound off and radio on will confirm, that the brain is quick to transform any music into a soundtrack. Maybe this is the explanation" (p. 214).

People are constantly involved in "cognitive shorthand" associated with filling in the blanks, making assumptions based an sometimes cursory perceptual input, and relying on frame of reference as they form attributions and strive to make sense of others around them. Although this dynamic is the basis of stereotyping, it is not necessarily bad or wrong.

If it were not for this cognitive shorthand, people would become extremely frustrated. It is not necessary or even valid to try to stop the process. Rather, the idea is to understand the dynamic and to avoid or reduce errors whenever possible.

The process of attribution formation I have described is inevitable, and it significantly influences communication whether in the home, at school, or in the workplace. For example, you might communicate more warmly with a student in the future if you attribute her behavior to being unlucky, as opposed to being lazy. You might communicate more respectfully with a faculty colleague because you perceive him to be bright and lively, as opposed to being a "squeaky wheel." Most certainly, *The Wizard of Oz,* in the communication involving Dorothy and her crew, was profoundly influenced by the group's collective attributions concerning the "great and powerful Oz." Witness how their perceptions, and subsequent communication, changed after the wizard's cover was blown.

What with problems associated with fuzzy language, invalid attributions, and pitfalls of using cognitive shorthand in general, it is a wonder that communication hits the mark as often as it does. But what of online communication? To all of the challenges outlined thus far, online communication carries additional burdens. These additional "lions and tigers and bears" can quickly sink instructors who might otherwise communicate well in a traditional classroom.

Online Communication: A Horse of a Different Color

Online communicators are particularly prone to communicative difficulties and complexities outlined thus far because online communication excludes rich and significant cues on which people normally rely as information sources. In this regard, it is noteworthy that communication researchers have consistently found that nonverbal cues are the dominant source of meaning in interpersonal communication (Mehrabian, 1972). Yet, these cues are missing online. As a consequence, online communicators are compelled to "fill in the blanks" more frequently than they might when face to face, leading to the potential for faulty prototype formation and invalid attributions discussed previously.

The added communication complexities of online can quickly lead to anxiety and hostility, feelings that might be excessive to what would normally be experienced in face-to-face interaction. Exchanges can quickly blow entirely out of proportion. People can come out of "left field" with surprising and often insulting language. Onliners refer to this type of communication as *flaming,* defined as electronic messages or retorts that express startlingly blunt, extreme, and impulsive language. A flamer often says things online that he or she would never say to another person face to face.

Misunderstandings of language or faulty attributions usually lie behind every "flame." A student receives a message open to interpretation, lacks the nonverbal inputs necessary to help interpret message appropriately, assigns faulty attributions to the message, and fires back with anger and name calling in the classroom. I will talk about solutions to this particular dilemma shortly.

Here are a few other differences between online and face-to-face communication of which you should be aware:

- *Individuals in computer-mediated groups are relatively more uninhibited.* Flaming is only one outcome of this dynamic. Online group members are also more willing to disclose personally sensitive information about themselves relative to face-to-face interaction (Siegel, Dubrovsky, Kiesler, & McGuire, 1986). The intimacy that can spring up within the virtual classroom is amazing. Students often comment that they quickly come to know their virtual classmates much better than coworkers and neighbors, even when the latter relationships have been of long duration.
- *Status differences play less of a role in an online environment.* The fact that a person is "The Instructor" or "The Boss" or "Knows What She Is Talking About" has less of an inhibiting effect on interaction (Sproull & Kiesler, 1992; Harasim, 1988). Some of the most successful online programs in the United States are adult centered and emphasize a facilitative, rather than professorial, instructor approach in the classroom. Instructors who are accustomed to the traditional lecture method and a "professor as God" dynamic will be surprised by the cheekiness of online students.
- *Interaction in online groups tends to be more evenly distributed among group members* (Kiesler, 1984). This aspect of online education is a huge advantage. I have often had students comment that they engage in online classroom discussion to a much greater degree than when in a traditional classroom. "Squeaky wheels" get shut down online because everyone has equal access to the instructor and to interaction in the virtual classroom.

- *Online consensus decision making takes significantly longer than when group members interact face to face* (Kiesler, 1984).   It tends to be more difficult for online groups to reach agreement. This dynamic significantly affects group projects. It can be tough for groups of more than three students to efficiently complete their work. Oftentimes, they must resort to conference calls on the phone. For this reason, when assigning membership for student projects, I like to assign students to work in dyads.

The balance of this chapter provides information useful for constructively dealing with the dynamics of online communication described to this point.

The WRITE Way to Communicate Online

Acronyms are helpful for remembering useful concepts. I like to use the following acronym, based on a bad pun, which is helpful whenever I engage in online interaction: the WRITE way to communicate online. The WRITE way involves communicating online in a manner that is (W)arm, (R)esponsive, (I)nquisitive, (T)entative, and (E)mpathetic. Here's an explanation of each component:

(W)armth

Words on a screen are two dimensional. Reading these words in isolation of nonverbal communication cues lends itself to "coolness" that can lead to overreaction and flaming. In this regard, online communicators sometimes lose perspective—acting as though messages are going into the relative privacy of a text file saved to the user's hard drive, rather than being downloaded and read by perhaps hundreds, even thousands, of people. People, in turn, read two-dimensional words in isolation, misinterpret fuzzy language, or experience faulty attributions, and react. Pretty soon it's—BOOM!—flaming communication that leads to embarrassment, chagrin, guilt, shame, and anger. In short, it is a whole plethora of potentially counterproductive human emotions.

Increasing warmth online does not have to be "touchy feely"—giving people the electronic equivalent of sloppy hugs and kisses. Rather, increasing warmth means to decrease the psychic distance among communicators. Being warm online is a way of reminding others (and you) that it is people who are engaged in communication, not software. There are several effective ways in which to improve online warmth.

1. Use the telephone when necessary. Phoning a student to clarify a point, or to negotiate a particularly sensitive issue should occur when e-mail just does not cut it. Some onliners think electronic messages should suffice for all communication. I do not agree. An occasional phone call can be useful. Its efficacy can be seen in a common revelation that occurs when two onliners speak together for the first time. Invariably, when I phone my students, the first thing we discuss on the phone is the fact that "real people" are behind the words on the screen.

2. Send sensitive information to private mailboxes. It is usually much more helpful to offer "constructive feedback" privately. This approach is akin to offering feedback behind closed doors.

3. Incorporate warmth into written text. Professional writers are able to convey a wide range of emotions. It is much tougher for mere mortals to do this. I have found it helpful to write occasionally about my family and interests. Sometimes, I might tell a joke, though the joke needs to be a "sure thing" because humor can easily backfire online. Example of a "sure thing" joke: Q: What has two knees and swims? A: A two-knee (tuna) fish. (Sorry for that—the opportunity was there and I just couldn't help myself.) Interesting examples and metaphor also sometimes work well. For example, I have had a lot of fun trying to relate this chapter to examples from *The Wizard of Oz*. Hopefully my struggle to find connections has also been interesting for you.

4. Describe the setting from which you are writing, or the weather or music to which you are listening. Online warmth of this kind helps students place you in a human setting.

5. Play with language. This suggestion adds warmth and contributes to understanding as long as it is not overdone. One way to have fun with language and symbols online is to use an occasional *emoticon*. Emoticons represent a way of bringing so-called nonverbal cues into online communication, though, technically, emoticons are not "nonverbal" communication because they are intentional and symbolic.

   My favorite emoticons are the smiley and winky: :-) ;-). The former emoticon conveys intended humor; the latter that the writer is poking fun in a nonthreatening way. An occasional frown :-(is okay as long as the receiver of a message understands the dissatisfaction is not being directed at him or her. I have also sent an occasional bouquet of roses: --<-<@ --<-@ --<-<@ --<-<@.

   I recommend that you use emoticons only as an occasional seasoning. A steady diet gets irritating as well as confusing. Does the emoticon that follows really look like *The Wizard of Oz* tinman to you? [:|]

(R)esponsiveness

Online communication is usually asynchronous. This means people can wait several days before getting a response to a message. The waiting period itself can feed into invalid attributions, many of which are negative ("Chad hasn't replied to my message! Hmmm.... guess he doesn't really think much of my ideas").

A solution is to set deadlines, or otherwise be consistent, in terms of when you give feedback. This reduces anxiety and creates an expectation on the part of students of when they should hear back from you. Once this expectation is satisfied through timely provision of feedback, trust—a positive contributor to warmth—will be reinforced. Try to return personal messages as soon as possible, and set up a regular rhythm of communication for other responses. Interestingly, instructors who upload feedback to students on a regular schedule—for example, by noon every Saturday—tend to get better student evaluations than do those who get feedback to students more quickly, but who are also inconsistent, getting papers back sometimes the next day, sometimes three days later, and so forth.

Another aspect of responsiveness is redundancy. Remember to provide occasional reminders to students. Think of issuing reminders as a proactive type of responsiveness. An interesting aspect of online communication is that it is possible to have a perfect memory of what was "said." Unfortunately, it can also be difficult for students to remember what is said when it is buried in thousands of kilobytes of information that have blasted through the class. Consequently, do not be surprised if students fail to act on an online request or forget, particularly if information is part of a larger message or part of a succession of messages on related topics. The use of short messages and redundancy helps to allay this problem and keeps online communicators on track.

(I)nquisitiveness

Defensiveness is reduced if people ask questions rather than make statements. It is usually more constructive to ask a person *why* than it is to tell a person *what.* Inquisitiveness serves two important purposes: Besides reducing defensiveness, it often provides information that is useful for solving a problem, resolving an issue, or whatever. Bringing valid information to bear on online communicative exchanges is almost always a good idea.

The attribution by Glinda the Good Witch that Dorothy was a witch missed the mark, but her timely question, "Are you a good witch or a bad witch?" secured information that saved the day. What would have happened if Glinda and the Munchkins had assumed Dorothy to be a bad witch and had attacked her? She never would have learned about the Wizard of Oz, the yellow brick road, or the Scarecrow, the Tinman, or the Cowardly Lion.

(T)entativeness

Defensiveness is reduced when people hear or read, "It appears that . . . " as opposed to, "It is . . . ." Inquisitiveness and tentativeness work well together. A question—framed in a tentative manner—reduces defensiveness and can also contribute valuable information (e.g., "Don't you think it'd be better if we . . . ").

Use tentative language and posturing with students, unless the situation dictates otherwise. The concept of sending "I-messages" rather than "you-messages" works as well in online writing as it does in oral interaction. It is often better to say or write, "I believe . . . " rather than to say or write "You are . . . . "

Sometimes, instructors must make absolute statements. You must occasionally send "you-messages." Communication with students and others might otherwise degenerate into a sloppy, gooey, indeterminate mess not unlike conversations that occur when a bunch of counselors get together to talk out a problem. :-) When to be absolute and when to be tentative is up to you. It is a judgment call.

(E)mpathy

An important aspect of online communication is to put yourself in the shoes of your audience. Always consider the position of your students. A wide variety of issues should be kept in mind. For example, a student can be a highly effective, intelligent contributor in the virtual classroom even if he or she misspells words or uses poor grammar. What if this student speaks and writes English as a second language? I tend to cut such students some slack in informal classroom discussion, though formal assignments must still be of a high caliber.

Sometimes students send e-mail excuses for tardy work or offer all types of interesting reasons for failure to perform. Some of this communication should be taken with a grain of salt. However, I do not have a problem with working with students who experience occasional difficulty associated with their schedules. I figure students choose to attend online for good reasons that often pertain to hectic lives. It would be contradictory, besides being decidedly unempathetic, to put the hammer down on these students without some consideration.

Empathy also involves inquisitiveness. I have always found it helpful to be inquisitive if I need information to better understand my audience. Ask a lot of questions if necessary. Gathering valid information helps reduce the likelihood of invalid attributions and prototype formation in online communication.

To summarize this section, the WRITE Way to online communication involves communicating in a manner that is (W)arm, (R)esponsive, (I)nquisitive, (T)entative, and (E)mpathetic:

- (W)armth means to use the telephone when necessary, send sensitive information to private mailboxes, and incorporate warmth into text.
- (R)esponsiveness means to set deadlines, or otherwise be consistent, in terms of when you give feedback, and to provide occasional reminders.
- (I)nquisitiveness means to ask questions. This allays defensiveness on the part of others, and collects information that might improve attributions and understanding.
- (T)entativeness means to use tentative language and posturing, unless the situation dictates otherwise.
- (E)mpathy means to put yourself in the shoes of your students and to perhaps cut them some slack from time to time.

Online Netiquette: Follow the Yellow Brick Road!

Proper form—following the rules—is important in most human undertakings. Among a gazillion examples of this are good table manners, proper greetings, and the effort taken by Dorothy and her troop to properly prepare for meeting the great Wizard of Oz. Online communication has its own protocol. Some learn it the hard way, by being flamed in a public forum when they goof. Even long-time onliners occasionally slip up and get roasted. In the interest of helping you avoid this unpleasant experience, I conclude this chapter with advice based on a 1994 post concerning "netiquette" from *Time Magazine's* website. All of these kernels of wisdom work well in the classroom as well as in general online communication:

- *Keep your posts brief and to the point.* A variation on this piece of advice is to use short paragraphs. I am not sure where I learned this tidbit, but a lot of short paragraphs are decidedly easier to follow on a computer monitor than is one "screen buster."
- *Encourage students to stick to the subject of a particular thread or classroom discussion.* Occasionally, you will run into a classroom full of exu-

berant students who genuinely like one another and want to talk about everything. You may want to consider setting up another electronic meeting as an outlet for classes that are particularly chatty. If your conferencing software precludes this option, then you may have to play traffic cop to keep discussion focused on course material.

- *If you are responding to a message, quote the relevant passages or summarize it for those who may have missed it. Do not copy in the entire message to which you are replying unless it is short.*   Conferencing software tends to paste in the entire message to which participants are responding. This means that users have to consciously go in and remove irrelevant portions. It is important to remind students to do this. Otherwise, too many unnecessary kilobytes end up in the virtual classroom.
- *Never publish private e-mail without permission.*   I occasionally respond in the virtual classroom to a private student query. However, I do this only if a student's question is innocuous and when my response needs to be read by the student's classmates. Sometimes, students need to be encouraged to direct their questions to the classroom, rather than to the instructor's private e-mail address. Obviously, truly private messages need to be kept private.
- *Discourage students from posting test messages or cluttering up the virtual classroom with "I agree" and "Me too!" messages.*   Participation can be an important component of an online class. To the extent that this is true, the question of how to define participation invariably pops up. Students need to be encouraged to upload substantive replies to course-related messages. I address the "Me too" and "I agree" approach to participation by discussing this problem in my course syllabus. I also gently address this issue in private student feedback to the extent it has occurred during the week.
- *Do not type in all caps.* (IT IS RUDE AND IS LIKE SHOUTING!)   I have one exception to this rule: I employ caps when grading student papers. Red pencils do not work in a word processor, but uppercase works great. The use of uppercase letters and asterisks helps to **SEPARATE** instructor comments from the text of student papers.

A Concluding Thought

It would be great if one could simply tap ruby heels and instantly be whisked off to the Kansas of effective online communication. The reality is we must start over with each new student group; and the communication dynamics discussed in this chapter are relentless and relatively unforgiving.

I have not found any shortcuts, with the possible exception of phoning each student early on. Such communication provides students with the information helpful for improving attributions of their instructor, though it does not help with attributions of classmates. If you have the time and other resources, calling each of your students might be a good idea. Doing so is still a relatively clunky "solution," however.

Someday, technology may improve to the point where online instructors can take off the straitjacket of the WRITE Way and other comparable, disciplined approaches to online communication. Until then, we must compensate.

I wish you well.

References

Feldman, J. M. (1981). Beyond attribution theory: Cognitive processes in performance appraisal. *Journal of Applied Psychology, 66,* 127–148.

Harasim, L. M. (1988). *Online Group Learning/ Teaching Methods* (Technical Paper #7). Education Evaluation Centre, The Ontario Institute for Studies in Education.

Kennedy, H. (1997). Rainbow in the dark. *Guitar World, 17,* 214.

Kiesler, S. (1984). Social psychological aspects of computer-mediated communication. *American Psychologist, 39,* 1123–1134.

Mehrabian, A. (1972). *Tactics of Social Influence.* Englewood Cliffs, NJ: Prentice-Hall.

Siegel, J., Dubrovsky, V., Kiesler, S., & McGuire, T. (1986). Group processes in computer-mediated communication. *Organizational Behavior and Human Decision Processes, 37,* 157–187.

Sproull, L., & Kiesler, S. (1992). *Connections.* Cambridge, MA: The MIT Press.

3

TALKING THE TALK

Humor and Other Forms of Online Communication

ARLENE HISS

The purpose of this chapter is to discuss how online facilitators should "talk" to their students. As Chapters 1 and 2 emphasized, carefully chosen words and expressions help make online teaching a positive experience for all involved. This chapter examines specific forms of online "teacher talk," conventionalized ways of communicating and writing in the online instructor role.

Teaching online is unlike any other educational experience. Faculty and students have to rely solely on the written word. There is no body language or eye contact to depend on as in the onsite classroom. Teaching online is also quite unique. Because online instructors at the University of Phoenix are dealing only with the written word, it is not possible to determine race, ethnicity, physical characteristics, physical challenges, or, in some cases, gender. For example, I mistakenly thought a student was a man based on the written communication in the classroom. There were no clues such as this person claiming to have a wife or husband. Four weeks into the class, I discovered he was a she.

A variety of components to "teacher talk" will be discussed in this chapter: *control talk*, *humor*, *special language*, and an *"andragogical" approach* (see Knowles, 1978). The facilitator who fails to pay special attention to these areas will run into difficulty.

(*Note:* I should mention here that rather than refer to descriptors such as *teacher* and *professor*, I will use the label *facilitator* throughout this chapter because effective online instruction is facilitative; effective online instructors guide classroom discourse with only a minimum of traditional lecturing.)

Control Talk

Usually, the idea of controlling a process has a negative, even dictatorial connotation. That is not the way it is meant here. *Control talk* refers to any communication used by an online facilitator to set tone, to clarify expectations, and to convey meaning that is understood by all. I will begin with a discussion of *tone*.

Communicating online can be sterile, which, in turn, can intimidate new students. Such students have never experienced the virtual classroom; they often need a lot of handholding. The first experience a new online student has often determines his or her likelihood for future success. Consequently, the first facilitators students encounter in entry courses must have a good working knowledge of conferencing software in order to help new students find their way. They must be extremely responsive to each student's problems and needs. The facilitator needs to have a caring persona rather than one that is cold and aloof. Messages sent by facilitators should come across naturally, as though they were speaking to students face to face. Students, in turn, will tend to model the facilitator's communication style, contributing to a warmer classroom environment.

An online facilitator should never be sarcastic. Sarcasm opens up a plethora of problems as students follow suit. Also, it is important to reread your messages so as to soften any questionable statements. Overall, in terms of establishing a supportive classroom tone, a good motto to live by is: When in doubt—don't.

As Chapter 2 observed, sometimes a "flame war" occurs. Flaming involves online conflict that erupts into personal or rude attacks. A facilitator who leads emotionally charged classes—such as, say, a course dealing with managerial ethics—might experience flame wars more often. There is a multitude of viewpoints whenever one deals with personal morals, personal values, and personal ethics in the classroom, many of which are potentially upsetting.

Though skillful online facilitators carefully craft responses to help extinguish flames, ideally, they set a tone that avoids the likelihood of conflict. Prevention is key. Some students are strong-willed and unbending in the virtual classroom. Effective "control talk" by the facilitator helps to chill out such students before they build up a head of steam. In this regard, a private e-mail or phone call to a particularly volatile student can also be a good idea.

Facilitators should not become irate or "lose their cool" when dealing with flames. In some cases, the flame war can be diffused with humor. If an entire class is involved in conflict, a note to the whole class is in order. It is important not to overreact to flaming, an approach that can easily create even more negative reactions from the students. By using calming language and by not dwelling on negatives, the students will usually move on. Do not ignore flames; but do not overreact.

Much of the time, a facilitator does not need to say or do anything when flames engulf the online classroom, because students will constructively handle the situation on their own. Such a happenstance can be a great learning experience, one that prepares students to better work within teams in the real world.

In short, the way the online facilitator communicates to the class sets the tone—how the facilitator goes, so goes the class. Students get their cues off the facilitator. A sarcastic or rude facilitator might very well produce a sarcastic and rude online class. In addition, a facilitator who is not very "visible" will likely have students who are also invisible. (Facilitators should post notes regularly to the class and their names should appear frequently.) And if a facilitator uses humor, students will also feel comfortable expressing humor. (More about online humor will be discussed later.)

Interestingly, effective online control talk can be indirect; it is often subtle. A carefully timed question to the classroom might help restore order. If online students are chatting excessively, a facilitator might set up a separate chat meeting or opportunity. In this instance, one of two things happens. Either students constrain chit-chat within an appropriate venue, or they take the hint and cut down on chatter. Either way, it is a win-win situation.

Effective "control talk" and other facilitating behaviors online help to set a productive tone in the classroom. It also helps facilitators to clarify expectations and to create a structure that contributes to learning. Here are some tips that relate to online expectations and structure:

Top Ten Hints for Success

1. Encourage online students to contact the systems operator (sysop) if they run into technical difficulties. The sooner technical problems are solved, the better.
2. Remember the 4-F motto. Be *Firm, Fair, Flexible,* and *Fun!*
3. Reply to student autobiographies with a personal note about something the student said. Online students love to be warmly welcomed.

Talk about their dogs, children, hobbies, or anything not related to work or school.

4. Have your syllabus ready to go at the beginning of an online course and be sure it clearly states when all assignments are due and the points or percentage of the grade for each assignment.

5. Always have class materials (e.g., lectures) uploaded the day prior to the first day of the classroom week, or whenever you previously said materials would be uploaded. Be consistent!

6. Always get back to questions from your online students as soon as possible, but no later than 24 hours.

7. Never leave your online class for an extended time without telling students when you will be back. If, for some reason, you cannot get through online (computer crash, etc.), contact the sysop or school immediately so they have the opportunity to inform your class of the problem.

8. Try to send students a handout, message, thought for the day, or *something* every day. Online students need to know you are there. One idea is to shorten longer uploads into handouts that can be submitted periodically during the week.

9. Give feedback and grades on a regular schedule every week. Online students hate not knowing how they are doing. Send grades and feedback frequently and periodically, on a regular schedule. Always provide some positives in your feedback.

10. *Maintain your sense of humor!*

Humor

A student of mine once said, "Humor belongs.... It enhances any experience, including learning, when the brain dumps 'crazy chemicals' into the body." When people are laughing, their brains seem to operate more efficiently and symmetrically. Laughter equals relaxation. A person cannot simultaneously laugh and be tense.

Humor in the workplace has recently become an important topic in management publications such as the *Harvard Business Review, Wall Street Journal, Training Magazine,* and *Business Week.* Management consulting firm Robert Half International reported that in a study of personnel directors at 100 of the nation's largest corporations (Roueche, 1996), 84 percent report that people with a sense of humor are more creative, less rigid, and more willing to try new ideas and methods (Roueche, 1996). Hodge-Cronin and Associates, a management consulting firm in Rosemont, Illinois, regularly conducts surveys on humor in the workplace. In their 1994 study, *Humor in the Workplace*, they surveyed approximately 600 top executives from various-sized companies and found the following:

- One hundred percent of the executives responding stated that humor has a positive impact in a business situation.
- Ninety-five percent of the executives stated that all things being equal, they would more likely hire a candidate with a sense of humor.
- Eighty percent of the executives stated that humor can have a positive effect when dealing with foreign executives, provided one understands the culture and uses the humor appropriately.
- Forty-three percent believed that the use of humor is decreasing yet the demand is increasing.

One of humor's most widely promoted benefits is that humor appears to fulfill an individual's need to be part of a group, an important consideration in the technologically dependent and *deindividuated* environment of online learning.

In addition, humor promotes novelty, divergent thinking, creative problem solving, and risk taking. The *incongruity theory of humor* helps explain how an individual is able to find an unexpected or novel way to approach a problem using a sense of humor. When something is incongruous, it does not fit a person's conceptual patterns and ordinary ways of looking at things. Humor gives people a way to distance themselves from the incongruous and to benefit creatively from the new ideas. *In other words, as an online instructor, you can help your students learn and help prepare them for the workplace by using humor in your classes.*

Obviously, there are many benefits to using humor in the online classroom. Humor warms up what might otherwise be a cold and sterile environment. Students need to feel comfortable with their classmates, facilitator, and the environment so that a positive learning experience can occur. According to Hill (1988), laughter in the classroom is a sign that students enjoy the learning process rather than viewing it as dull and boring. A smile can come right through the computer monitor via your words. A smile shows openness and enthusiasm. Appropriate humor generally brings the facilitator and students together. I personally like this motto: Laugh and learn.

Humor also eases stress for the online student. New students are typically nervous and highly stressed when they first enter the virtual classroom. Once students are made comfortable, perhaps by laughing at a funny anecdote or a topic-related humorous story, their anxiety lessens.

Humor should never be a substitute for substance, however; rather, it should serve as a "seasoning" that enhances the online learning process. A lecture that is sprinkled with topic-related funny stories will be remembered for a long time to come. Look for amusing anecdotes that can be used to illustrate difficult concepts and for analogies that transform abstract ideas into more familiar examples. Students comprehend material better when it is related to a funny story (Hill, 1988). I ask new students to relate a positive and a negative learning experience from their pasts. Nearly half of them list a facilitator's sense of humor as a positive. Student end-of-course surveys also reflect the positives associated with a facilitator's sense of humor.

The following story is an example of humor that might happen in an online logic class that will serve the purpose of establishing a more informal tone:

> The professor writes the following to his online class in logic:
>
> "By way of introduction," the professor began, "let me begin the course by posing a question. Suppose two men were digging a well. Upon completion, they come out of the hole, and one is clean while the other one is dirty. Which man will go and take the shower?"
>
> Several students responded:
>
> "The dirty one, of course," one student typed.
>
> "Really?" wrote the professor. "Remember, they can only see each other, not themselves."
>
> "I see, now," responded another student. "The clean one sees the dirty one, assumes that he is dirty, too, and takes the shower."
>
> "I see we have a lot of work ahead of us," types the professor. "How could two men be digging a well, and one of them not get dirty?"

A group that laughs together stays together. An online class that can have fun together will be more cohesive and, in turn, inclined to be more productive. A group that laughs together shares a common experience. Laughing is like yawning, it is contagious (Hill, 1988). Here are a few other suggestions:

- *One-liners are great for loosening up an online class.* Think funny! Online communication gives the advantage of the time to think of a snappy comeback. An online student might kiddingly ask me to "forget about assigning a final paper." My comment back might be, "In your dreams, bucko!" Rather than make a boring statement such as "You bet" or "That is true" to a student comment, I might say, "You can bet your cowboy boots on it." Small and seemingly insignificant tweaks can change a boring statement into a humorous one while still saying the same thing. My favorite is when students will share that one of the reasons they like online so much is because they can go to school in their pajamas. My response to that is, "You wear that much?" I like to tell the students that this is the only "clothing optional" university around and that they do not have to worry about makeup or bad hair days.

- *Self-effacing humor can work well.* When online facilitators laugh at their own mistakes, rather than cover up or make excuses, this sends the message to students that the facilitator is human and that it is okay to make mistakes once in awhile. Hopefully, students will feel comfortable about laughing at and learning from their own mistakes.
- *Have a folder full of funny stories that relate to a particular topic under discussion.* Here are a couple of my favorite funny stories that I use when discussing resistance to change:

> Humor has a very significant role in defusing resistance to change. There will always be somebody who sees the negative side of change, such as the old farmer getting his first look at a new car. He watched as the proud new owner cranked and toiled to no avail. The old farmer kept repeating to all who would listen, "It ain't gonna start." Once it started and the driver jumped behind the wheel, his message changed: "You ain't gonna be able to stop the thing!"

> An efficiency expert was hired to go through a company and make recommendations for changes. He went into the plant and to the first worker he saw standing by a lathe, he said, "What is your job around here?" The worker said, "To be honest about it, I have nothing to do." From the plant, the efficiency expert went upstairs to the office staff, spotted a woman sitting behind a typewriter, and asked, "What is your job around here? What do you do?" She said, "To be frank about it, I really don't have anything to do." "Ah Hah!" he replied, "Duplication!"

Online humor can be effective when used well, but it is also risky. People love to laugh and, if you can make them laugh, they will generally listen to what you have to say. However, if you, as an online facilitator, are uncomfortable with using humor, they should not force it. And, needless to say, but I will say it anyway, humor should *always* be G-rated. Any facilitators should stay completely away from any racial, ethnic, gender-related, political, religious, gay, or alternative lifestyle humor.

Not all humor works, so a few words of caution are in order . It is a mistake to confuse professionalism with seriousness. You should take your education and teaching seriously, but take yourself lightly in your online classes. On the other hand, do not make your classes a comedy club. Misplaced humor can be destructive and distracting from the topic at hand. The best philosophy is to laugh hard and to work hard.

Online students need to realize that a sense of humor is a skill that they can and should develop to enhance their learning and their opportunities in the workplace. But sometimes humor can detract from a serious message or discussion. It is important to find a balance. It is up to you to set boundaries when using humor and to ensure that humor is limited and appropriate. It is easy to be misunderstood online. What you intend to be humorous, another party might see as offensive. Consequently, use *emoticons* to convey meaning—for instance, if you send a message intended to be funny, be sure to include a smiley :-). Tease gently with a winkey ;-). Many facilitators resist use of emoticons (they are not true nonverbals) but their use can make the difference between constructive humor and destructive misunderstanding. The next section continues the discussion of emoticons and their use.

Special Language

When onsite facilitators are face to face with students, they can use nonverbal expressions to communicate in conjunction with words. Online communicators, however, must depend solely on words. Therefore, it is relatively more challenging to strive for clarity. The facilitator cannot afford to be as vague or ambiguous as in an onsite classroom. I try to communicate online just as I would if a person was facing me, plus I might add in a few emoticons to clarify my meaning. Emoticons come from several sources. It is not necessary to use even a fraction of them. In fact, I use the smiley and winkey almost exclusively. Here are some of the more creative emoticons:

:-)	Humor
:-))-:	Masking theatrical comments
:<)	For those with mustaches
:<)=	For those with mustaches and beards
:/)	Not funny
P-)	Pirate
(@ @)	You're kidding!
:-"	Pursing lips
:-v	Just another face profiled from the side
:-V	Shout
:-r	Bleahhh (sticking tongue out)
:-)	Smile

:-D	Laughing smile
:-*	Kiss
;-)	Wink
:-X	My lips are sealed
:-P	Blahh [slip of the tongue]
:-|	Indifferent
:-(	Frown
:'(	Crying
:-o	Oh!
0:-)	Angel
\ \//_	Vulcan salute
->>>>>--	Feather (just teasing, tickling)
()	User is sending cuddles
{}	User is sending hugs
@-`-,--	A rose for you (this one has thorns!)
|_|}	Cup of coffee (or other beverage)
)-I	Wine glass
>-I	Martini glass
]-|	Champagne glass
_}]	Beer mug
}-I	Margarita glass
(-:	User is left-handed
%-)	User staring at a green screen too long
[:]	User is a robot
8-)	User is wearing sunglasses
B:-)	Sunglasses on head
::-)	User wears normal glasses
B-)	User wears horn-rimmed glasses
8:-)	User is a little girl with a bow in her hair

From time to time, online communicators may use abbreviations as a "special language" to convey meaning:

FB	Files busy
Sysop	System operator
BRB	Be right back
BTW	By the way
CP	Copy protection
FUBAR	"Fouled" up beyond all recognition
FWIW	For what it's worth
FYI	For your information
gr&d	Grinning, running, and ducking

IAE	In any event
IMO	In my opinion
IMHO	In my humble opinion
IMNSHO	In my not so humble opinion
IOW	In other words
OIC	Oh, I see
OTOH	On the other hand
ROTFL	Rolling on the floor, laughing
RSN	Real soon now
RTFM	Read the [fine] manual (or message)
SNAFU	Situation normal, all "fouled" up
TIA	Thanks in advance
WYSIWYG	What you see is what you get
BBL	Be back later
CUL8er	See you later
<g>	grin
<grin>	grinning
<smile>	smiling
GMTA	Great minds think alike
J/K	Just kidding
LOL	Laughing out loud

Another effective online technique involves communicating naturally in a conversational (as opposed to academic) tone. From an online perspective, this is "special language" because in a very technically dependent learning environment, there is a special need to avoid academic jargon that sometimes finds its way into a traditional classroom. If facilitators type as they talk, their communication will come across as being warm and friendly. (*Note:* I have used this approach in writing this chapter.)

Finally, the online medium has developed special labels that also constitute a "special language." Lectures are often called any number of names online. The most common one is *lecturette*. There are many facilitators, however, who do not care for either the term *lecture* or *lecturette*. They coin new names such as "Thoughts from Toni," or "Hiss-a-Grams," or "Shuey's Shoebox." This gives a less formal feel to what is actually a lecture, and contributes to online facilitation as I defined it earlier in this chapter.

An interesting term used by some online communicators is *lurking*. As ominous as it may sound, lurking merely means someone is observing a class but is not participating. *Lurkers* are hidden from sight. For this reason, from an ethical standpoint, it is vitally important to announce any lurkers to your classes.

Here are some other terms that are technical in nature and specific to online classes. Several of these terms relate to virtual academic programs that use particular software as a conferencing system. Nevertheless, the principle underlying the term can still be applied to other platforms. Rather than list these terms alphabetically, I have listed them by relationship:

Meeting Room: A bulletin board meeting room open to those who have been invited.

Branch: A meeting room that has been branched from a main meeting room. All people who are in the "meeting room" will receive an invitation to join the "branch."

Read-Only Meeting: A meeting created to be "read-only," so that only the creator can write to that room. Such a meeting might work well as a "lecture hall."

Attachment: A note can be sent attached. By doing this, all formatting remains intact; longer notes can be sent; graphics, charts, photos, spreadsheets, and PowerPoint slides can also be sent this way. However, attachments may carry viruses, and it is not possible to reply to an attachment, so they should be used only when necessary.

Text File: A file saved in ASCII that does not include any control symbols used in word processing to format paragraphs, to italicize, and so forth. Most online communication is sent as text.

Notes/Messages: Notes that users send to one another and to meeting rooms.

Reply: When a person sends a return note or responds to a message that has been received.

Logon: Connect via modem.

Upload: Send mail out.

Download: Receive mail in.

Sysop: The system operator is the person or department to contact if facilitators or students have technical questions or problems.

Onsite: Classes that are held in real time in a physical classroom.

An "Andragogical" Approach

In recent years, some educators have begun to distinguish between *pedagogy* that relates to traditional education and *andragogical* approaches that are adult centered. Even if an online classroom is populated with teenagers, the virtual medium requires student discipline that presumes a high level of maturity and a facilitator approach that presumes he or she is leading adults.

One of the biggest mistakes an online facilitator can make is to treat the students as children. A facilitator who "talks down" to students or patronizes them can expect problems. Another area that spells trouble for facilitators is to communicate as though they are the only experts in class.

An adult-centered perspective assumes that students can bring a wealth of information and experience to a class. In many cases, adult online students may be as knowledgeable as the facilitator in a particular area. The facilitator should make such students feel comfortable about sharing their expertise without the threat of being reprimanded or ridiculed. A facilitator might do this by asking questions that draw on student experiences and knowledge, and then the facilitator can bounce off student responses by contributing other information and insight. I have found that when an online facilitator says too much or otherwise dominates discussion, adult learners have a tendency to clam up. They are inclined not to want to disagree with the "expert."

Another way to utilize the expertise of adult learners is to create assignments that ask students to teach other students a topic with which they have knowledge. Online students are then able to discuss, debate, learn from each other, and take away new ideas that did not come exclusively from the facilitator.

Conclusion

Teaching online can be a wonderful and rewarding experience to the extent that (1) facilitators are warm and caring and not afraid to have a sense of humor; (2) they carefully choose words in order to constructively control classroom processes related to the environment, dialogue, and tone; and (3) they talk *to* students and not *at* them. There is special language to learn and to use, and the need to presume a high level of self-discipline and maturity on the part of students.

Learning to use these elements of online "teacher talk" is like learning to ride a bicycle. Once a facilitator successfully captures the parameters of teacher talk in day-to-day facilitating, its nuances remain and will hold across a wide variety of online instructional challenges. I hope my observations help you to get in the virtual saddle and to have a smooth and enjoyable ride. : -)

References

Hill, D. J. (1988). *Humor in the Classroom.* Springfield, IL: Charles C. Thomas.

Knowles, M. (1978). *The Adult Learner: A Neglected Species.* Houston, TX: Gulf, pp. 48–59.

Rouche, S. D. (Ed.). (1996). Humor's role in preparing future leaders. *Innovation Abstracts, 19,* 20.

4

THE STORY OF ONE LEARNER
A Student's Perspective on Online Teaching

LORRAINE PRIEST

The purpose of this chapter is to introduce the topic of the online student's needs and how online instruction can best respond to those needs. My focus is on the challenges faced by the online student—educationally, physically, and emotionally. In order to accomplish the purpose of the chapter, I discuss three main topics. First, as a way of introduction, I offer some background about myself and about why I chose online education. Second, I share some of the necessary characteristics of the effective online learner, characteristics that include high motivation, independence, active learning, good organizational and time management skills, self-discipline, and adaptability. Finally, I describe the needs of the working adult online learner, including suggestions about teaching practices and attitudes, and how online programs and teachers can help adult learners succeed in the online classroom.

Background of the Online Learner

In many ways, my story is like that of most students. I went through the public school system, including high school, and did pretty well. I got average grades, attended regularly, and enjoyed the socializing. But something happened. Unlike other kids, I dropped out. Why? I don't really know. Maybe it was partly because I was not born into a scholastic family.

Neither of my parents had a high school diploma, so education was not stressed. In some ways, it felt sort of natural for me to drop out of high school. No big deal.

Fortunately or unfortunately, depending on how you see it, dropping out of high school did not prevent me from getting jobs. In fact, I had many jobs—working in a factory, gluing soles on shoes (I didn't *stick* with this job too long :->), working in a screen print shop (laid off due to lack of work), and working in a lab, looking through a microscope eight hours a day (gave me headaches). I finally ended up as a cashier in a retail store.

I did well in retail. I even advanced to the position of office manager. But then the reality of no high school diploma hit. It turned out that I could not advance in this retail organization because of my lack of education. At that time, I thought that was really unfair. Previous to this job, I had been married and had a beautiful little girl. But that marriage ended in failure and my life had taken a complete turnaround. I had become the breadwinner of the family. And, as a single parent, I needed to step up to my financial responsibilities.

Cashiering was not going to pay enough to support my daughter and me. I had thought this was going to be the job of my dreams, but the needs of a 2-year-old raised the ante. It became necessary to move back to my parents' home so that they could watch my daughter during my working hours.

I needed to get a better job and make more money. I left the cashiering position for a job in the automotive industry. The auto industry paid more and it did not require me to go back to school while working on the assembly line. But it was at this time that I became fully aware that I was going nowhere without an education. That was clearly brought home by the fact that anytime I was offered a promotion, the opportunity was taken away the moment it was learned that I did not have a high school diploma. I was offered a promotion as a supervisor, but the company required that I get a general equivalency diploma (GED) certificate.

The decision to continue my education became necessary. I scrambled to the local high school and took my GED test. My manager gave me two weeks to show them the GED certificate before completely turning me down for the job. At the time, I considered him the "pushy type." He constantly nagged me about getting a formal education to further my career. He had his master's degree and he was not going to let up on me. But I guess that was the kind of motivation I needed—I got my GED certificate and immediately signed up at a local college and began to earn a bachelor's degree by attending class on Saturdays and Sundays.

Then the obstacles to furthering my education grew. The company closed its facility and my hopes of completing a bachelor's degree quickly faded. To complicate matters (in sort of a good way), I had met a wonderful man. We married and moved our new family to another state, much to the dismay of my educational goals. There, the pressures to improve really increased. The firm worked out a transfer for me, but then moved me to a new facility, where it seemed like all my associates and fellow employees had master's degrees. I really felt like I did not fit in. In fact, without a bachelor's degree, job opportunities and advancement were definitely not open to me.

To add to the challenges, I was faced with another dilemma. My new job took me on the road a lot and all the local colleges required me to be physically present in classes—not an unreasonable requirement, but one that left me out of the program. Besides that, the closest college was too far away for me to work and travel to school at the same time. I was at my wit's end.

Then I heard about the University of Phoenix's (UOP) Online Campus. A fellow employee had read about UOP in an ad. Both of us were impressed that even though online education was new, the University of Phoenix's online program was accredited. It seemed that the program could enable me both to return to school and get a legitimate degree.

The UOP program looked to have many positive factors for a person in my situation. For example, another advantage of the online classroom seemed to be that it allows for quiet and shy students to say things and speak freely about a subject. Those students can express hidden talents that may be masked by the face-to-face contact in a traditional classroom. I am one of those students. I was always concerned about my eastern accent. The idea was attractive to me that online, my accent, as well as many of the features people would normally see and hear in a traditional classroom, would be gone.

Despite the apparent advantages, I called UOP with significant skepticism. Keep in mind that this was 1992 and online education was an area that many people felt was not feasible. One did not hear much talk about the Information Highway or the Internet. I can clearly remember people telling me that there must be a lot of online cheating going on when students take tests or exams. I heard the words *diploma mill* more than once. As a result, I spent many hours struggling with questions like: Is online education real or a false front? I wanted flexibility, but I also wanted a real education.

I am now very happy to write that the decision was positive for reasons that I will explain later in this chapter. But I can say now that two years later, the sound of my name being called up to receive my bachelor's degree was a dream come true. I even delivered the graduation speech for my class in 1994. And that was only the beginning. I decided to keep going and earn my master's degree, as well. As a direct result of the flexibility and quality education offered by the Online Campus, I learned that I was up to the challenge and could do it. In another two years, I made a second trip up to the podium and received my master's degree.

The moral of the story? Despite all the obstacles that life, family, and worked placed in front of me, online education offered me a chance for success. I am now the only person in my family with a college degree and I feel it is an honor beyond any of my expectations. Thanks to the online option, the dream continues.

As a direct consequence of my online education, my employer has given me responsibilities that only a person with a degree would normally have. As the operations manager for two mainframe computer systems, I am currently implementing a client/server reporting application in the United States and making the necessary preparations to implement it globally. With each degree came an increase in pay as well as an advance in my position within the organization. I am also responsible for the security of the company's data and work with outside vendors who would like to interface electronically with my company. I am given these responsibilities because I have the educational background and skills that show that I can manage assets and resources, and that I have the ability to make decisions and resolve problems.

Characteristics of Effective Online Learners

It was not only the online program that helped me to succeed. As a working adult learner with experience and motivation, I had the characteristics for success. I found the online option a perfect fit, but not everyone will. The online environment allows motivated adult learners to return to the classroom and overcome the obstacles that prevent most working adults from attending a traditional college.

Originally, I looked at online education as being simply convenient and easy to access. But I soon learned that the online environment is challenging because it changes a person's way of thinking. In my exchanges with other online students, I was exposed to how other people handle ideas and problems. The online medium helped me expand my knowledge by bringing me together with other people. It provided a way of learning that gave me new insights and alternative methods for handling problems that I could not learn alone.

It is exactly because of such possibilities and challenges that the online medium is not for everyone. In fact, because the Online Campus is set up for working adults who wish to further their education but are not able to attend a traditional classroom, it does require commitment and particular characteristics of the learner. Although online learners do not have to be computer experts or have a complete understanding of the software, they do need a willingness to learn.

In one of my online classes, I was introduced to the ideas of Ronald Gross, an authority in lifelong learning and adult education. I think Gross (1977) describes the characteristics of the successful online learner to a tee when he outlines some "basic truths" about learning and growth that can strengthen the educational adventure of adult self-development:

- They take command of their own learning, master more things, and master them better than those who rely on being taught. They tend to have greater zest for learning and make better use of their time.
- They learn differently than children. As working adults, online learners have a different sense of themselves, of their time, and of what's worth learning.
- Adults tend to take responsibility for their own learning. Online learners are able to tailor learning for themselves, not just accept something ready-made.
- How well online learners learn depends, to a great extent, on their temperaments, circumstances, needs, tastes, and ambitions. Success in learning depends not so much on the subject itself (or maybe even on the medium) as on the learner's own engagement.
- Virtually (not a pun) every aspect of the adult online learner's life—work, leisure, personal relationships, community activities—has the latent power to enhance his or her learning, but only if the adult learner can find or create the ways to utilize it.

In other words, the working adult who decides on the online alternative needs to take personal responsibility for his or her learning.

Many people think that online education is an easy way out. I let those people know that if a person is planning to attend an online class, he or she must be self-directed. Online is a tool to assist those who are unable to enter the traditional college classroom but are motivated to meet their educational goals. As working adult learners, online students bring their goals, experiences, and desires to learn to the classroom. They are motivated to bring something new to each and every class. They are prepared to succeed.

Needs of Online Learners

There are ways online programs and teachers can help the working adult online student to succeed. First, the online student needs support services. When I first started in the online program, I needed support in understanding how the university functioned and how it related directly to me. The way of doing this that worked for me was having the same person handle my school problems from the start. At the UOP Online Campus, I was able to contact an enrollment counselor who helped me get through those first few classes. She was knowledgeable and always willing to assist, no matter what the problem. In one instance, I needed help in getting transcripts from another college. This was all new to me. Having a familiar voice at the other end of the telephone made the task easier. I still had the same fears that most new online students have when they start a class— What will the teacher be like? What type of work will he or she expect? Will the teacher follow the syllabus or will it be different?—but those fears were tempered by the reassuring presence of an online guide.

Second, the online learner needs a social context for learning. Working adults may be self-directed, but they also value the exchange of ideas and meaningful relations. It is particularly important that online programs address these two issues. I suggest that online programs give their students the opportunity to follow the progression of classes in such a way that they will find themselves in classes with the same people, what has been referred to as *learning communities*. I found that in doing so, I was able to develop close relationships that enhanced my own learning. It gave me a chance to get feedback from people I trusted about how much I learned throughout my program and how other people were struggling with concepts and issues.

In addition, online instructors should take advantage of possibilities for group work. Much of my most valuable learning took place in UOP study groups, cooperative groups of three to six students who work together for the duration of a course. Onsite study groups meet out of class, but online study groups create separate electronic meeting places where they can build a unique way of responding to course objectives and assignments. By sharing information and resources in groups, online students can achieve more and increase their capacity for self-assessment. I understand that there is some controversy regarding the use of online study groups and that study groups are not appropriate for every online course, but I also believe that online instructors should take advantage of this tool when and where they can.

Third, the online student needs to experience effective online communication and teaching practices. From my experience, online instructors require a special sensitivity because of the unique experiences of the new online student. Online instructors must be prepared to deal with many technical problems that face the new student. They do not have to fix the problem all the time, just be understanding and know where to refer the student. For example, new online students are sometimes unable to figure out why their homework is not reaching the instructor even though they have read the manual. The online teacher needs to be prepared to assist the student and send detailed instructions to him or her.

There are other times when an online student is trying to explain a technical problem and the instructor needs to probe for information to get to the real cause. If a student continually tells the instructor that he or she is sending in homework but it never reaches the classroom, the right questions can soon tell the instructor that the new student has the instructor listed as a "meeting" rather than a "person." Or the teacher might discover that a student using Microsoft Works does not fit into a Microsoft Word class. Online instructors do not have to know everything about all kinds of hardware and software, but they do need to know how to ask the right questions. Even if online students have a great deal of support available, they want to look directly to their instructors for help. If online instructors are willing and able to help, they can create a special bond between the online student and themselves.

Online instructors must also give the online student a means to contact them other than via the computer. In many cases, online students with technical difficulties have been required to call the university help desk with a problem because they are not able to contact the instructor. Online students should be encouraged to contact the instructor directly by phone if there is some reason they cannot communicate online. Many times, an instructor will tell students to leave a note, but if the student's computer is not working, they cannot leave a note. They have to call.

Fourth, the online student needs clear guidance through the online curriculum. Because the current online course is typically all verbal, words must be used effectively. When an online syllabus is prepared, it should be particularly clear and detailed. A detailed explanation of when assignments are due is better understood by the student when both the week and the due date of an assignment are referred to rather than just writing "The assignment is due on Saturday." Syllabi should contain a full description of what is expected when the student is to give feedback to the class. Rather than just tell students "A summary is due every week," instructors should tell them exactly what is expected of them in the assignment. The clearer the syllabus, the less likely online instructors will have students coming back and saying, "Oh I thought you meant...."

Fifth, online students need tolerance for differences. Online instructors must be prepared to deal with many different types of people and social conflict. The online environment is a diverse place. Many times, something written may be misinterpreted; instructors need to be able to intervene effectively while not disrupting the flow of the class (see Chapter 12). When online instructors see the classroom going in the wrong direction, they need to intervene appropriately. Often, it is simply a matter of clarifying the situation by directing a note to the class—something like, "Oh I see this was mentioned in a response. This can have many meanings...." Online instructors should neutralize or defuse a situation as it arises, not after students are "flaming" each other. This sometimes requires that the instructor have a private conversation with an online student.

Sixth, occasionally an online student needs extra motivation. The online instructor will have to deal with the unmotivated working adult and/or group. If there is an online student who is not performing, sending a direct note is usually sufficient. But these kinds of situations must be handled carefully. It can be embarrassing if everyone knows that "something" has transpired between the instructor and a student. In addition, when a group does not perform, it is partly the responsibility of the instructor to make sure that it does. One effective means of encouraging an active class is to require that a conversation be related to the topic at hand. Instructors can help online students stick to the topic by asking questions that explicitly require students to relate a particular conversation to the subject under discussion. Encouraging students to talk about how this week's readings apply to their work environment can also stir up some conversation and keep the online learning process on track.

Finally, an instructor should let the online students know that he or she can and does track attendance in class.

Conclusion

For working adult students, the online method of teaching and learning can far surpass any traditional method. Online students want to get more out of a class than sweating out a final exam. They want practical knowledge and meaningful social interaction. They may be self-directed, but they also want the guidance of a facilitating instructor. If done right, the online experience can instill confidence in students and earn the recognition of others. In short, online education can give working adult students, who might not otherwise have the opportunity, the taste of reward and the personal fulfillment they never expected.

Just as online education is not for all students, it is not for all teachers. Online education is still about dealing with people, and effective online instructors need the skills to do so. They need to be able to communicate and write clearly. In the end, the challenge of online education remains the same for online instructors as teaching remains for all teachers—to share their knowledge, time, and hearts with students.

Reference

Gross, R. (1977). *The Lifelong Learner*. New
York: Simon and Schuster.

5

RESHAPING TEACHING AND LEARNING

The Role of Liberal Arts in Online Education

BILL PEPICELLO AND ELIZABETH TICE

In this chapter, we argue that the role of the liberal arts within any institution of higher education goes beyond the content of specific courses. Specifically, we will explore two major functions the liberal arts can serve in the online environment. In many respects, the traditional roles of the liberal arts curriculum can be replicated in online courses and programs. For example, the primary learning activities in any literature course consist of reading, writing, and group discussion—whether the discussion occurs orally or through text is irrelevant.

The mission of the liberal arts is essential to online education, particularly in the areas of basic skill assessment and integrating those basic skills across the online curriculum. The liberal arts is both a set of content areas encompassing the sciences, humanities, and social sciences, as well as a set of processes providing a platform of basic skills in support of general college curricula. In the online environment, the role of the liberal arts is confounded by the parameters imposed by a primarily textual mode of communication as well as the attendant skills and proficiencies necessary to succeed in the medium, but there remain many possibilities. For example, although many online programs are primarily text based, the application of new technology allows for exceptional graphics capabilities. This means that even liberal arts courses with a heavy visual element (Art History, for example) can also be adapted to the online environment.

The liberal arts can provide the foundation for the necessary basic skills to achieve online success. Of particular importance are online assessment of writing and math skills, and the development of basic skills across the online curriculum, particularly in the area of general education processes such as critical thinking and problem solving.

Online Proficiency Assessment

Basic proficiency in English and math is critical to your success not only at the University of Phoenix, but also in your professional life. It is our goal to help you gain the basic proficiencies in math and English that you will need to be successful in your undergraduate studies and, later, as a college graduate. (From the Home Page of the Online Proficiency Assessment System Website)

In the areas of basic writing and math skills, the online environment offers the opportunity for institutions to utilize assessment tools that not only address the skills necessary for general online student success but also skills required for particular programs (e.g., undergraduate business or nursing) and professional life. From our experience at the University of Phoenix (UOP), a comprehensive approach has (1) an online proficiency assessment system and (2) online remediation systems.

An Online Proficiency Assessment System

Historically, students entering an educational program are given a timed, closed-book examination to assess their current skill bases. In many traditional settings, such a paper-and-pencil exam can be logistically daunting. Consequently, changing assessment to an online format can more efficiently facilitate the process and help institutions maximize their assessment resources. Examples already exist: Standardized, national exams, such as the GMAT, have moved into an electronic delivery system.

Of course, one challenge posed by online assessment is to replicate the security of exams without the necessity of onsite controlled environments. Although more and more, traditional assessment formats are being replaced electronically, they are still offered in controlled environments such as campus computer labs. One solution is a randomized test bank. It requires more work to create and to calibrate numerous test items, but randomized testing allows students to test and retest as necessary, each time facing a new set of questions. Recent technology can be programmed to grade written responses to essay questions from both a conceptual and a grammatical stance. Integrating randomized test items with automatically graded essay questions allows a complete assessment process to be achieved online.

In addition, there are many educators who argue that a computer cannot assess particular skills. For example, some believe that the only comprehensive way to assess student writing performance is through an onsite essay exam graded by an experienced English professor.

On the other hand, although we understand how this perspective appreciates the complexities of evaluation, we point out a couple alternatives. First, much of what occurs in the evaluative mind of the professor (especially when it comes to the standard rules of grammar, punctuation, and sentence structure) can indeed be programmed into a computer program. Second, it is also possible for the exam to be completed in an online environment with the computer scoring the objective portion and a faculty member evaluating the subjective elements.

As a workable example of an online English and math assessment system that addresses the preceding issues, we offer the online Proficiency Assessment System, developed by the School of General Studies at the University of Phoenix (UOP). The University of Phoenix is the largest private university in the nation, with more than 60 physical campuses and learning centers from Hawaii to Puerto Rico. It also has as a burgeoning online student body.

All UOP undergraduate students must demonstrate basic understanding of English and math skills. Each proficiency requirement must be met by one of the following methods:

- Achieve a grade of C or better in COMM 215: *Essentials of College Writing* and in MTH 200: *College Algebra I;* or
- Pass the English and math College Level Examination Program (CLEP) exams; or
- Pass the University's English and math proficiency exams.

The University's School of General Studies is responsible for supporting skill assessment of these incoming undergraduate students in the varied locations and modalities. For years, this was done with a paper-and-pencil exam. There was a testing administrator at each campus and incoming students were required to come to a controlled Testing Center for testing in math and English. Online students were required to find a proctor to act as intermediary and the time-consuming process included multiple mailings. The actual exams were created by UOP faculty members, normed to national exams (such as CLEP), and distributed by the School of General Studies. Any change in even one test question created the need for mass redistribution and replacement, creating numerous logistical problems.

As the University of Phoenix grew, it became more and more difficult to manage the paper-and-pencil process. As a result, UOP decided to pursue an online solution to student assessment. The result is an online proficiency assessment system (PAS). This system was created to provide UOP students with 24-hour-a-day access from any Internet connection. Students can take the exam when it is convenient for them. All registered UOP students access PAS through hyperlinks to the University's webpages. An automated registration system checks student identification numbers against the database of registered students and allows authorized students immediate entry. New students, whose ID numbers have not yet been added to the database, are manually verified and granted access within 24 hours. Once registered, students have unlimited access to the system. When an online student enters the PAS, they are advised to do the following:

- Register by clicking on "Go to Class."
- Click on "New Users" on the registration page.
- Follow the registration instructions carefully.

Only registered students of UOP may enter the PAS and it may take up to 48 hours from a student's initial attempt at registration to gain access to the system.

Once within the PAS system, students find two separate and very important services. First, the Skills Enhancement Center (SEC) helps students review their skills and prepares them for the proficiency exams. Students can brush up on English and math skills before they take the proficiency exams. The SEC provides interactive English and math tutorials that test student understanding through questions and quizzes. Students can take an entire tutorial or select a specific area that includes a review of the basic concepts covered on each exam and a practice exam. Practice exams mirror the real exams and give students a good idea of their level of preparedness. If students have taken algebra and composition courses in previous coursework, the review and practice provided by the SEC helps them succeed on the real exam.

The online PAS is crucial to the University of Phoenix, where the majority of undergraduate students enter the university with more than 24 units of transfer credits. Many of them have taken basic algebra and composition courses and do not want to repeat these courses. The SEC allows them to brush up on their skills so that they do not have to retake entry courses as well as allows them to enter advanced courses with the necessary skills.

Second, the actual math and English proficiency exams are located in the Testing Center. When students are ready to take the exam, a simple click on the Testing Center button allows them to begin their testing. Students then have two opportunities to take each of the exams. To enter the Testing Center, students must accept the Testing Agreement. Each entry is also considered an attempt at an exam, so students are discouraged from entering the Testing Center until they are ready to take an exam.

We understand that not all institutions have the technological resources to create a PAS type of system. Still, others might have partial capabilities. Fortunately, the beauty of online technology is that an institution can mix and match systems and still present a seamless program to students. For example, an in-house instructional technology group down the hall from the School of General Studies created the SEC even though it did not have the technology to create the randomized exam needed for the Testing Center. For that, we went to Chariot Software in San Diego, a company specializing in web-based testing systems. Chariot not only created the testing portion of the system but it also supported the system on Chariot's own server for a very reasonable monthly fee. Consequently, when a UOP student in Livonia, Michigan, clicks on the Testing Center button in PAS, he or she is immediately linked to the testing server in San Diego.

Nevertheless, despite all the advantages of PAS, we still recognize that online testing allows greater latitude for student cheating. Our experience with a six-month beta test, however, demonstrated that student pass rates for the online exams followed the same trends as the paper-and-pencil exams. We interpret this as partly meaning that if students were cheating in significant numbers, the data would reflect higher pass rates. Research conducted by Chariot with other institutional partnerships indicates the same outcome. Safeguards are necessary, however. The exams are timed in such a way as to make the test a closed-book exam. Students are allowed only two chances to pass each exam. In addition, a number of other characteristics are built into the system to preclude student cheating. As discussed earlier, the exams are randomized. Once students have entered the system, their activities are tracked, making most cheating possibilities highly unlikely. If a student goes into the exam to print a copy of the questions, the entry is counted as an attempt. A student can memorize the answers to one set of questions, but the next entry will generate a whole new set.

It seems that the only reasonable way for a student to cheat on the proficiency exams is to have someone else take the exam. Although this is possible, it is not as simple as just taking the test. In the end, unless the accomplice is willing to write all of the student's papers, the truth will eventually become apparent. As one George Mason University instructor has pointed out (Benning, 1998), "Certainly, cheating is pervasive...it's deadly obvious. The introduction [of an essay] will be written in broken English; then it will have this flawlessly written, almost doctoral-quality body; then a conclusion that goes back to broken English."

In this regard, we do remind students that they are responsible for creating an appropriate and honest testing environment. We make the following suggestions:

- Tell students to use resources only during the tutorial phase and to remember that the exam is designed to demonstrate what they know
- Tell students to find a quiet room, free from distraction, in which to take the exam.
- Tell students to make sure that they schedule the appropriate amount of time to take each exam.

The PAS system does require that students have the requisite software capabilities. Microsoft Explorer 3.02 or Netscape 3.02 is required in order for students to properly run the exams and the tutorials on their computers. Students can download a free copy of these browsers. Students must also check with their Internet provider to make sure that they will have adequate time to utilize PAS. Getting timed out of the exam can be avoided by coordinating with an Internet provider before students enter the Testing Center. Students can learn how to extend their inactive time to one hour so that they have the time to complete an exam.

Finally, the testing engine includes a complete back-end data management system. Administrators at each local campus can enter the system to see testing results of their particular students. Results of the testing identify areas of student strengths and weaknesses, and allow counselors to place students in the appropriate courses. Central administrators can see data on all students. From the administrative side, the system allow extensive opportunity to report on testing trends, perform item analyses and export the data to the Institutional Research Department. Also growth occurs, the system can be expanded accordingly.

Online Remediation Systems

Online entrance testing and test preparation tutorials alone cannot provide a full complement of services in the enhancement of a student's basi skills. Many students need support in basic skills as they progress through their chosen course of study.

Online remediation systems must also replicate their traditional counterparts. There is a large commercial market for electronic (CD-ROM based) remediation programs, but many schools with large online populations are creating their own specialized tutorials for remediation of basic skills. This allows educators to customize the learning to focus on the specific skills necessary for success in their respective programs. Technology also allows for online writing labs, once held in the basement of the English Department, to be managed efficiently through electronic conferencing and e-mail. With well-developed systems, online students can enjoy a high level of support in the basic skills from the comfort of their own computers.

The University of Phoenix Online Campus offers its students a free math and English tutoring service. The service is advertised on a monthly basis in an electronic bulletin board meeting called "Student Lounge." The services of online math and composition faculty members are made available to all students in all programs. Online students need only to send their papers and math questions to a "math tutor" or "writing tutor" mailbox. Although this service does not take place in real time, a student often receives help within 24 hours. The School of General Studies is developing a similar "Virtual Writing Lab" service that will be offered to all UOP students.

Liberal Arts across the Online Curriculum

Another important role of the liberal arts in the online environment is the development of a comprehensive curriculum that nurtures such basic areas as communication and thinking skills. Instruction in a professional program is, by its nature, narrowly focused. The objective of an accounting program is to produce good accountants. Nursing programs focus on producing competent nurses. Liberal arts courses are aimed at developing within students a depth and breadth of general knowledge that can be applied to educational and professional settings. The general outcome is to provide students with the perspectives necessary for meaningful self-examination of personal and social values, as well as enhanced ability to understand and cope with social, technological, professional, and cultural change.

Likewise, the role of the liberal arts at the University of Phoenix's Online Campus is to provide a balance to the specificity of professional programs. Liberal arts instruction focuses on the development of skills of communication and critical thinking in order to enable online students to function as well-rounded members of society. To this end, the textual environment of the Online Campus curriculum serves a liberal arts purpose—it makes online faculty and students aware of the nature of written communication. It is commonly known that written language has all kinds of (sometimes arbitrary) rules that can be found in style guides and grammar books. It is also general knowledge that written language is much more formalized and restricted than the spoken word. In this sense, textual language is a "dialect." If fully utilized, the online medium offers a built-in emphasis on written communication that sensitizes students to the nuances of language and how language affects the way people deal with other people.

In other words, if the textual environment of online education is utilized in interactive ways, it can facilitate a multiplicity of perspectives and at the same time the need for critical thinking and problem solving. Consequently, the Online Campus promotes critical thinking through student interaction (as opposed to a correspondence course model) by exposing students to new ideas and to individuals whose critical thinking skills are more fully developed than their own, and by helping students to structure these contacts and their ideas (Brookfield, 1986).

Such an online liberal arts approach must be intentional. The UOP process began in many ways during an online student competencies conference facilitated under the auspices of the University of Phoenix. One issue concerned how to define critical thinking so that it would translate equally to online communication; the topic was discussed at length. The goal was to arrive at an operational definition of critical thinking that cuts across UOP's onsite and online settings. It was generally agreed that *critical thinking* is the ability to synthesize knowledge and experience, and then use that synthesis as a tool for the analysis of new situations. More specifically, it was agreed that the identifiable and measurable elements of critical thinking include the following:

- The ability to identify a problem
- The ability to identify a reasonable set of solutions
- The ability to apply an appropriate solution

As a result of intentional reflection, onsite and online UOP students with little previous college experience are required to begin their studies with a course entitled *Skills for Professional Development*. This course, which introduces students to the liberal arts and general studies, not only covers academic skills such as writing but it also exposes students to such important liberal arts processes as critical thinking and problem solving.

Skills for Professional Development provides core liberal arts competencies and structured learning experiences that help the online learner make the transition back into the college classroom. Content areas include critical thinking skills, interpersonal skills, intrapersonal skills, study skills, adult learning theory, online group process skills, time-and stress-management skills, writing skills, problem-solving skills, and information on personal learning styles. The course also helps online students develop onsite and online library research skills.

In a typical week, online students in *Skills for Professional Development* might be asked to do the following:

- Analyze personal reasons for returning to school.
- Identify possible contributions to an effective learning environment.
- Identify writing strengths and areas for improvement.
- Discuss stages of group development.
- Identify advantages of the UOP study group process.
- Identify and demonstrate effective online learning techniques.

As you will note, all three of the identifiable and measurable elements of critical thinking mentioned previously can be found in the content and activities of the one week in the course. In addition, it illustrates how an online program can promote educational outcomes that go beyond technical competency and how the goals of liberal learning can be achieved by emphasizing the interactive and group capabilities of the online medium.

Unquestionably, professional schools such as the University of Phoenix and its Online Campus share several common goals with liberal education. Joan S. Stark and Malcolm A. Lowther, professors of higher education at the University of Michigan, and colleagues identified these common goals, all of which are reflected in UOP's *Skills for Professional Development* course (Stark, Lowther, Hagerty, & Orczyk, 1986). They include the following:

1. *Communication competence.* Online students are expected to be able to read and write and use these processes effectively to convey ideas and information. Communication skills are essential to professional practice and growth, and although a weakness of the online medium is in the area of speaking skills, a strength is reading and writing instruction. For example, *Skills for Professional Development* teaches a writing process that involves five steps: planning, drafting, revising,

formatting/proofreading, and publishing, emphasizing the transition from academic to practical writing.

2. *Critical thinking.* The UOP onsite and online student is required to examine issues rationally, logically, and coherently. Although critical thinking is a universal desired outcome, professionals particularly need a repertoire of thinking strategies that will enable them to acquire, analyze, synthesize, and evaluate information. This is accomplished in *Skills for Professional Development* by having students analyze case studies in study groups. Case studies are not only related to the educational experiences but they also include issues related to the workplace. For example, a typical case study concerns members of a UOP study group who are not contributing, easily translated to other types of work teams.

3. *Professional identity.* The UOP student in *Skills for Professional Development* is concerned about improving the knowledge, skills, and values of the profession. For example, a library skills activity in the course requires students to use a library's periodical index resources to identify articles published in professional journals in such topics as international copyright protection, public support for the arts, and U.S. high school graduation rates.

All educators, onsite and as well as online, must be watchful to make sure students do not neglect the liberal arts. To ensure that UOP's professionally trained graduates also have the broad critical awareness traditionally expected of educated persons, the university institutionalizes the liberal arts through means such as the *Skills for Professional Development* course, and continues to explore the common ground between liberal and professional education, and between liberal and online education.

Conclusion

Recently, much attention has been paid to the shifting paradigm of higher education in the United States. The heart of this shift is a movement from an emphasis on *teaching* to one on *learning,* a more student-centered and outcomes focus. These discussions point to the preeminence of the adult learner in the shift from instruction to learning.

Just as significant in this shift is the changing role of faculty in the teaching and learning process. As Robert Barr, director of Institutional Research and Planning, and John Tagg, associate professor of English, at

Palomar College in San Marcos observe, faculty members in the learning paradigm are partners with students in an environment that is cooperative, collaborative, and supportive (Barr & Tagg, 1995). Faculty members serve as content experts in the learning model, but they also serve as facilitators of learning, encouraging vertical strategies for student interactions that lead to academic success.

This shift has particular relevance for the liberal arts and the new educational technology represented by online education. Associate dean for Computing, chair of the Computer Science Department, and director of the Center for the New Engineer at George Mason University, Peter Denning (1996) discusses market and political forces that are motivating new educational templates. He calls on institutions of higher education to ask the hard question: "What do today's students want?" In his opinion, among the issues that higher education students wish considered are the following:

- A general education that affirms values central to civilization, cultivates historical sensibility, and prepares people for responsible and meaningful careers, families, and lives
- Professional education after the bachelor's degree
- Distance education and virtual universities
- Restructuring curriculum for the Internet
- Learning how to cope with the apparent rise of complexity in a world increasingly dominated by technology

Denning sees a student's "call for competence" in areas such as communication, analysis, history, managing teams, and operating a computer. This call is not only for technical proficiency but also for social proficiency—involvement and participation in community life, all within the purview of the liberal arts. The new university, as Denning sees it, has a business orientation, is professionally oriented in a way that integrates and validates liberal arts values, and is a student-centered learning environment rather than a presentation-oriented teaching environment.

The thoughts of Barr and Tagg, as well as Denning, are obviously relevant to online education. Their perspectives on the learning process translate perfectly to the virtual classroom. At the University of Phoenix's Online Campus, rather than simply transmitting information, a faculty member facilitates the learning process as an informed and practiced participant. The requisite set of talents for the learning paradigm faculty member, as with the online campus instructor, is not one focused on the traditional researcher and lecturer, but one focused on a more applied practitioner (i.e., a working professional with academic qualifications).

The liberal arts has always stressed that colleges and universities are not only purveyors of information but also purveyors of humanity, preparing students to communicate and to think productively in society. The online medium does not negate this basic function of general studies. In fact, as liberal arts educators, we must particularly enter the twenty-first century prepared to fulfill our traditional roles in highly nontraditional settings such as the online classroom.

References

Barr, R., & Tagg, J. (1995). From teaching to learning: A new paradigm for undergraduate education. *Change, 27* (6), 13–25.

Benning, V. (1998, October 5). Higher learning, lower behavior—Students cheat by computer. *The Seattle Times,* p. A7.

Brookfield, S. (1986). *Developing Critical Thinkers.* San Francisco: Jossey-Bass.

Denning, P. (1996, November/December). Business designs for the new university. *Educom Review,* pp. 22–30.

Leatherman, C. (1990, December). Definition of faculty scholarship must be expanded to include teaching, Carnegie Foundation says. *The Chronicle of Higher Education,* p. A1.

Stark, J. S., Lowther, M. A., Hagerty, B. M. K., & Orczyk, C. (1986). A conceptual framework for the study of preservice professional programs in colleges and universities. *Journal of Higher Education,* 57 (3), 231–258.

6

THE ELEMENTS OF EFFECTIVE ONLINE TEACHING

Overcoming the Barriers to Success

ANITA BISCHOFF

Students often choose a group-based online learning environment because they enjoy learning from other working adults. Their interest in learning is maintained when the instructor and other students share in their journey toward greater understanding of course topics.

As part of the learning model at the University of Phoenix (UOP), online students learn not only from their instructors, who provide content expertise and feedback to each individual, but also from other adult learners in the classroom. Instructors expertly facilitate discussions that help working adults apply the lessons from their texts and the instructors' lectures to their work lives.

When I speak at conferences on distance learning, academics often approach me afterward with some variation of "Sounds intriguing, but does it really work?" In fact, many express an interest in being trained to teach online so that they can see for themselves whether it works. Fortunately, my experience with the University of Phoenix Online Campus and research on online learning leads me to believe that asynchronous group-based conferencing is a highly effective tool for learning.

Recent research by the University of Phoenix's Institutional Research office indicates that online instruction is "every bit as effective as regular classrooms in serving working adult students in business and management programs" (Kauffman, 1996). Further, many University of Phoenix instructors of both onsite and online students argue that online students interact and learn at least as much, if not more, than other UOP students. They attribute this to the highly interactive online learning model, which encourages more regular communication with the online instructors and other students than usually experienced in onsite classrooms.

The key to online education's effectiveness lies in large part with the facilitator. While serving as director of Academic Affairs at the University of Phoenix Online since 1995, I identified certain competencies that directly enhance teaching and learning in a discussion-based online medium. By reading student end-of-course surveys each week, speaking with academic counselors, and talking to students at graduation each year, I found that an instructor's performance in the following areas seems to tie closely to perceptions of their effectiveness: (1) *visibility,* (2) *feedback,* (3) *materials,* and (4) *retention.*

Not coincidentally, the UOP training program focuses largely on these areas. Specifically, online instructors are taught to (1) maintain visibility, (2) give regular feedback, (3) provide high-quality materials, and (4) remove obstacles to student retention.

Even experienced onsite instructors need training, coaching, and mentoring in these areas to translate their effectiveness from the actual to the virtual classroom. Having seen how important these skills are, I am convinced that prospective online instructors should receive extensive training and mentoring in these areas before "flying solo." This training will prevent them from making avoidable mistakes that detract from their effectiveness as online facilitators.

As an added bonus, instructors who attain proficiency in the preceding four areas tend to receive the most positive feedback from their students and colleagues. They also enjoy the gratification and intrinsic rewards of helping students fully grasp the class objectives and progress toward degree attainment.

This chapter will focus on each of the topics mentioned, providing prospective, new, and experienced online instructors with a thorough understanding of the importance of each aspect of online teaching and how to attain proficiency in each area. In each of the following four sections, I will share a vignette or two to illustrate the significance of the topic, then generally discuss the components of each instructional competency. Finally, I will provide more specific examples and further explore the components that make up each of the four main areas of online instruction.

The Role of Visibility in Online Teaching

About a year ago, a new online teacher received negative feedback due to students' perceptions of his "low participation" in the class discussion. Students complained to an academic counselor that they only heard from the instructor at the end of each week's discussion. Since previous instructors had been more involved in class discussions, they wondered if their current instructor was lazy or uninterested. When their counselor suggested that they ask the instructor about their perceptions, the students did so with great trepidation, for fear of offending the instructor.

While taken aback at their criticisms, the instructor explained that he was trying to avoid dominating the discussion; thus, he read each day's notes with interest, but saved his own remarks until the end of the week. He further described how he summarized the discussion, analyzed it in light of his experience and the readings, and extended on the discussion to foreshadow the next week's lecture. The students agreed that his input was valuable, but pointed out that the relative sparseness of the input was discouraging to them, since they were used to more regular messages from their instructor.

The instructor finally realized what the problem was. The students could not "see" him reading notes and nodding his head encouragingly, or were not aware of his presence on days when he did not write to the class. When the instructor fully understood the dilemma, he agreed to write more notes to the discussion meeting during the week. Soon, the students perceived that he was "visible," and his consistent presence reassured them that they were progressing appropriately. The students felt gratified that their feedback had been taken seriously and that it resulted in a positive resolution, since the instructor's accommodation to their needs as learners made their class more interactive and rewarding.

Consider another example: During an online mentorship, an instructor-in-training with full responsibility for an online class suddenly disappeared for a few days. His mentor tried to reach him by computer and phone yet was unable to get any information other than that the trainee was out of town on vacation. By the time the trainee finally resurfaced days later, his mentor had already stepped in and saved the class from derailing. When asked for an explanation, the trainee described how he had gone on vacation to another city, expecting to load the conferencing software onto his host's computer. However, the host happened to have a Macintosh, so his Windows-based software was not compatible. Even after he officially failed mentorship and was denied admission to the online faculty, the disgruntled trainee could not understand why being offline and out of communication for a total of six days out of a five-week class was such a concern.

Lack of visibility and desertion of a class without communication to the administration does not bode well for an online instructor's willingness to put the students' needs first. Every online instructor needs to be aware of the various ways they can increase their visibility in their classes.

Online Visibility and Public Messages

The preceding vignettes point out that public messages are key to the perceptions of an instructor's presence. Similarly, since no one can sense someone's presence in an online environment, written messages from the instructor to students in the online class are necessary for students to feel connected in the online classroom environment.

On a related note, online instructors often do not realize that sending personal correspondence via the online medium does not substantially enhance their visibility. Namely, if instructors answer individual questions by replying to personal mailboxes, other students fail to see the interaction; that is why conducting as much class business as possible in the open forum is recommended.

What kind of messages does a visible instructor send? A sampling of the variety available and examples of each include the following:

- Content-related messages (lectures, handouts, clarification of points in the text, discussion questions, synthesis of discussion)
- Process-related messages (order of assignments, directions for sending assignments, description of the flow of the class, guidance when students become confused)
- Technical tips (software tips, information about how to send attachments, discussion of how to format notes, URLs)
- Protocol guidelines (code of conduct, plagiarism statement, netiquette, online tone)
- Responses (answers to student questions, feedback on work submitted to the meeting)

If students benefit from visibly seeing the instructors' notes in the online classroom, which messages are particularly effective in establishing visibility? Messages demonstrating that the instructor is actively reading the discussion often prove effective. ("Canned" messages, although at times necessary, are somewhat less effective in establishing visibility because they do not represent individualized responses, nor clearly reflect that the instructor is involved in reading and responding to this particular class.)

As one technique that enhances the instructor's visibility while adding content-related value, some instructors remove the name from a question addressed to the instructor's personal mailbox, share the question in the main forum, and answer it publicly to benefit others in the class who may have the same question. In fact, the question may be from a student in another class being taught concurrently or even from a student in a previous class. The origin of the question does not matter, as long as the sender's anonymity is protected and students benefit from the instructor's response.

Online Visibility and Modeling

Another benefit of instructor visibility is that the visible instructor is modeling how the discussion-based instructional model works. If students are required to write to class meetings a certain number of times each week, for example, I would argue that online instructors should maintain at least the same level of participation as the students.

Another key to setting a positive example is that an instructor modeling a high level of participation often motivates students to enhance their own participation. They know that the instructor demands their participation by observing the instructor's high participation level. On the other hand, when an instructor does not maintain an adequate level of participation, students may assume they have been given tacit permission to reduce their own levels of participation. They assume that their instructor will not feel comfortable confronting them or grading them down for the same behavior that the teacher is exhibiting.

Online Visibility and Reducing Isolation

A final reason that visibility is critical is to prevent a sense of isolation that distant students often encounter. If the students connect to the classroom once or twice a day, finding a number of new messages in the open forum each time, they feel reassured to be working collaboratively with their instructor as well as other students. If they fail to see a note that they expected (e.g., a weekly lecture), they learn to react and ask the instructor directly for the materials that are missing. The comfort felt by students whose instructors are visible cannot be underestimated in the distance education environment, where students do not have the trappings of the traditional university (e.g., familiar faces, student unions, and student activities) to provide a sense of belonging.

Ultimately, taking responsibility for being "visible" means that it is the instructor's responsibility to alert necessary personnel if anything occurs that would prevent the individual from fulfilling his or her contractual obligation. If an emergency arises, the instructor should follow the university's procedures in order to ensure that the students' learning will not be interrupted. Often, a substitute teacher is essential, due to the high need for instructors to be visible in the online classroom.

The Role of Feedback in Online Teaching

One neophyte online instructor whom I observed felt strongly that the university's focus on regular feedback, particularly evaluative feedback, was exaggerated and that it distracted from the learning process. He told students that they would hear from him only if they were "heading for trouble." Otherwise, they should assume that they were doing fine. Only when he received several furious student end-of-course surveys after his class did he realize that his practice, while understandable and consistent with his teaching style, was neither appropriate nor effective from the perspective of his online students. Students stressed that they needed regular feedback to know how their performance was judged, how they could improve, and how their final grade was calculated. The instructor discussed this situation with more experienced online facilitators and, with their assistance, adapted to his students' demands for substantive and frequent feedback.

Frequent and Consistent Online Feedback

Effective online instructors not only write to class meetings regularly but they also provide frequent and consistent feedback to the class as well as to individual students. Frequent and consistent feedback in the online classroom can stimulate active engagement by techniques such as questioning assumptions, disagreeing with certain points, and pointing out well-analyzed points.

Of course, these facilitation skills are not dissimilar to those of an instructor in a face-to-face classroom; yet, the frequency and consistency of feedback are even more necessary in an online classroom. Why? Online students cannot see their instructors or other students nod their heads, frown, look quizzically, or smile encouragingly. What is usually nonverbal feedback must occur through written messages, which makes online feedback particularly critical.

Giving feedback in the main meeting includes asking questions, suggesting alternative perspectives to consider, and extending on students' ideas. Feedback also includes answering questions in the main forum whenever possible, since many times the answer to one student's question may prove useful to the entire class.

Timely Online Feedback

Providing timely feedback within the class forum is important. Since an online class moves quickly, timeliness is essential to give students guidance and teach them the material in depth. Further, when guiding asynchronous discussions, the instructor needs to facilitate and foreshadow, instead of "catching up" with the discussions that have already been written and digested. Less timely feedback may lead to a perception that the instructor is not fully involved in the class, whereas timely feedback reassures students that the instructor is focusing on them and on their learning. Furthermore, feedback that is timely is far more motivational and beneficial to performance improvement than delayed feedback. Thus, online feedback is best when it is prompt.

Diplomatic Online Feedback

When feedback is provided to students in the main class meeting, diplomacy is essential. Since student motivation is closely linked to self-efficacy, well-worded feedback will encourage learners to continue in their programs and feel confident that they will succeed online.

Well-worded suggestions from the instructor are valuable not only for the student's learning process but they may also provide learning opportunities for the entire class. For example, gently pointing out the need to explore a theory underlying an opinion more fully may lead to the class's understanding that "gut feelings" are not convincing within the context of an academic discourse. The point can generally be made without undue embarrassment to the student who shared the gut feeling.

Occasionally, an instructor requests that students critique each other's assignments in the online classroom, usually providing guidelines for effective analysis to make the criticism constructive as opposed to personal or negative. When diplomatically worded, this type of feedback may also enhance the learning experience, since students practice the skill of receiving peer feedback as well as the skill of providing critiques to their peers in a written forum. I am convinced that setting the correct guidelines to ensure that students are supportive, as opposed to attacking, is essential to the success of this technique.

When the instructor needs to provide critical feedback to individual students, the feedback should be couched in a way that maintains the learner's dignity. If a student is exhibiting behaviors that are disrupting the learning process, for example, he or she will need to receive positive but clear feedback that the conduct is not appropriate. The wording (and private transmission) of such a message will help to avoid further disruption in the learning environment by reducing the chance of the situation escalating. A critical message may need to be rewritten several times before the correct tone and wording are achieved; however, this attention to diplomacy is far more likely to bring about the desired outcome than sending a less reflective message.

Evaluative Online Feedback

One online instructor whom I coached became increasingly frustrated when students asked how she calculated grades for the course. Having worked with elementary school students for years, she was not used to being challenged about her grading policies and procedures by students. Fortunately, through our discussions she realized that grading was part of teaching, and that doing it well would lead to more effective student learning. Further, by scoring students' work and tying it to the grading guidelines shared in her syllabus, she removed some of the ambiguity in her grading procedure and demonstrated to her adult learners that their performances matched the grades they earned. Additionally, after teaching more courses, she recognized that her students needed regular, detailed feedback during the course, not just a grade at the end. Fortunately, she no longer needed to answer frequent questions about grading, since her new procedures and guidelines were clear and consistent, thereby allowing relatively little ambiguity.

Evaluating students (covered more completely in Chapter 14) is an important part of providing effective feedback. As at any university campus, learning to grade fairly and effectively is a teaching skill that must be mastered by all online instructors.

Why should an instructor invest the time to provide detailed evaluative feedback to online students? Online students tend to have high standards for their own performances, especially if they are adult learners who have returned to school after succeeding in their work lives. Like any learners, they need to know where they stand in order to gauge how best to improve. Substantive feedback helps them perform at higher levels and thereby earn higher scores in subsequent courses.

Students in an online forum, perhaps because it is a relatively young learning medium, may resist accepting a grade given by an instructor, more than students faced with a similar situation in a regular classroom. This is even more likely due to the ease with which a student can send a quick electronic message, as opposed to the possible intimidation factor when addressing an instructor in person. Although often the most uncomfortable aspect of teaching, grading effectively is critical to student learning and effective online teaching.

What should an online instructor do to encourage students to understand the need for and utility of grades? When his students balk at his (particularly rigorous) grading practices, Douglas Beckwith, curriculum supervisor and faculty member for UOP Online Campus, compares the process of grading to that of evaluating employees. Discussing grading in this context seems to help set the right expectations and attitudes when students fail to recognize that grading is unavoidable in most programs, not to mention that the instructor is the authority when grading disagreements arise.

Completing a weekly grading summary with point values helps both the instructor and student recognize when a student needs help to succeed. If a student does poorly in a class and fails to improve with constructive weekly feedback, some advising may be necessary, such as a suggestion that the student consult an academic counselor.

Templates and Online Feedback

How is evaluative feedback delivered in an online setting? Universities establish their own guidelines and often articulate these in the instructor's contractual agreement. As an example, at the University of Phoenix Online Campus, specific feedback on assignments (including grades) must be provided within a week of the assignment's receipt. This specific evaluative feedback, as well as the use of weekly templates, helps students to understand how their grades are earned and to avoid surprises at the end of the course.

Experienced UOP online instructors have often attested to the value of using templates when providing weekly feedback to students' personal mailboxes. Each individual student receives a completed template that articulates the points they earned on assignments (out of total possible points), as well as points for each week's participation. A few sentences highlighting the student's performance, such as encouraging him or her to try harder the next week, are also highly recommended. Here is an example of a typical week's template:

Dear Jim:

Your point totals for this week are as follows:

    _06_   of 6 possible points for discussion

    _10_   of 10 possible points for participation

    _17_   of 20 possible points for the week's essay

    _06_   of 6 points for weekly summary

Your total is 39 out of 42 points. (Please use the past week's grading summary if you wish to compare your total points so far with the points possible and look up your grade so far in the course.) Also, let me know if you did not receive any of your assignments this week, as I returned them earlier this week with specific feedback and suggestions.

Jim, you showed a great deal of improvement in your participation levels this week, sending quality messages 6 out of 7 days this week, as contrasted with 4 out of 7 days last week. I particularly enjoyed message #57, in which you outlined a situation at work and tied it to the theories in Chapter 4 of your text. I hope that next week you will continue to participate actively, since your well-considered questions bring up important points and add to your peers' learning experience at this online university.

Warmly,

Jill B. (Instructor)

The Role of Instructional Materials in Online Teaching

A seasoned instructor, hurrying to upload the syllabus and the first week's lecture, failed to proofread online materials that she had used many times to teach the same course. The due dates for assignments within the syllabus included various dates in April, although the class was running in June. After asking the appropriate questions to correct the situation, her students still expressed a high level of frustration with the instructor, having perceived (correctly) that she did not take the necessary time to customize her materials for the current class. The embarrassment that resulted made such an impression on the instructor that she warned other instructors to revise their materials carefully, which likely saved others from similar mistakes.

Content-Driven Online Materials

Instructional materials include syllabi, mini-lectures, handouts, references to URLs and readings on the topic, assignments, discussion questions, examples, answers to assignments, and other materials that are either prewritten before the class begins or added during the class to enrich the content of the course.

Messages that are not content driven should be minimized, since discussions need to be focused on the class and noncontent messages may prove distracting to the topics being explored. Although an instructor's role is to facilitate, it is also to provide supplemental material that enhances the text and thereby helps students to attain a deeper understanding of the course and to meet the stated learning objectives.

Carefully Edited Online Materials

The content expertise that is infused into a written online lecture, along with the chance to see examples of other's materials, can lead to a higher-quality presentation than typically seen in traditional classrooms. If, however, the instructor does not edit the materials carefully, the result may be an embarrassing situation, as shared in the preceding vignette.

The ability to polish and improve class materials each time a class is taught is a huge advantage of online teaching over onsite. Of course, refining class materials demands that an instructor remembers to record when an assignment needs clarification or when a point demands more elaboration next time. For future classes, the ensuing modifications directly benefit students, who are the recipients of increasingly polished materials (often worthy of publication).

If the university uses modules or course materials that are appropriate for a regular classroom, the instructor may be called on to adapt the course to an online format. In cases like this, all of the oral presentations should be removed and group projects should take into account the time involved in coordinating group projects within an asynchronous medium. Modifications to an onsite module must be carefully communicated to online students in a timely fashion to avoid confusion.

Speaking with a colleague who teaches for another well-known online university, I asked how and when their curriculum developers adapted syllabi from the regular to online versions. She explained that the developers usually provided an online-specific version *after* publishing the onsite version. She also noted that the curriculum adaptations were not always successful, since the adapters were usually not online teachers, but editors. Once, in fact, the editors had missed something significant—proficiency in oral presentations was listed as a learning objective of a text-based online course. Even more tellingly, four group projects were due in a five-week online course. She and the other online instructors were forced to reedit the curriculum so that it would work online. As a result, they suggested to the administration that future syllabi be adapted solely by experienced online instructors.

An instructor teaching a course for the first time, whether onsite or online, may wish to contact previous teachers with curriculum questions or suggestions. At some universities, instructors are encouraged to share online syllabi and/or lectures as examples, although instructors usually develop their own lectures. This helps to personalize them and infuse them with their own content expertise.

Online lectures need to be concisely written, since they are not mere transcripts of oral lectures. Drawing on text readings, work experience, and outside sources, the online instructor crafts a thought-provoking and polished piece based on the theories covered in the assigned readings. Further, online lectures may conclude with two or three well-placed discussion questions designed specifically to promote critical thinking and stimulate the week's discussion in the class forum.

Last, since Web addresses (or URLs) change frequently, a careful instructor always checks the URLs thoroughly before sending up a lecture that includes Web addresses. (The rationale for the use of URLs will be more thoroughly covered in the next section.)

Copyrighted Online Materials

Instructors may be tempted to send full-text articles from newspapers or the Internet to their classes, particularly if they are accustomed to handing out copies of articles in traditional classrooms. However, the practice of sending full-text articles without permission from the publisher is legally prohibited except for rare instances.

When speaking at academic conferences, I encourage current and aspiring online instructors to share up-to-date and relevant materials by providing students with URLs instead of sending full-text articles to the online classrooms. This practice protects them and their universities from copyright issues.

Not only is the practice of providing URLs effective from a legal standing but it also encourages students to explore the Web. Students may be compelled to do further Web-crawling during or after looking up the cited articles, so the extra effort may prove helpful to their researching abilities.

As in regular classrooms, instructors may highlight and attribute short excerpts from published materials according to copyright laws. The 1997 booklet, *Questions and Answers on Copyright for the Campus Community,* by the Association of American Publishers, is an excellent resource for educators determining whether to cite a passage or refer students to URLs.

Orderly Online Materials

Posting materials on set dates helps students get into the flow of an online course and program. If the university prescribes these dates, the students move forward in their programs without needing to readjust to each new instructor's timing. For example, students may learn to expect a weekly lecture, depending on what the university requires. Similarly, they may anticipate that certain assignments, such as weekly assignments, are due on certain dates from course to course.

Other materials, such as handouts, need to be clearly highlighted by the instructor for maximum clarity and usefulness. Besides highlighting these materials, instructors may use branch meetings or otherwise distinguish the readings for clarity's sake. Further, students should be clearly informed whether reading each handout is mandatory or discretionary. This will enable the students to focus, organize, and manage their time and will support their success as learners.

The Role of the Online Instructor in Student Retention

A student whose personal and professional life hit rough patches at about the same time felt depressed and generally pessimistic about her online studies. While she had been doing well and making solid progress toward obtaining a diploma within a year, she felt that her focus was scattered and that she should "stop out" for a few months before returning to the university. She mentioned this to the instructor from whom she had taken her first online class. The instructor, who had been honored in the past for her teaching skills and commitment, spoke for half an hour on the phone with the discouraged student. Actively listening to the student's story, she asked questions such as, "How would you know whether the time was right to return?" She also asked about the student's online cohort, whom she might miss at graduation if she walked across the stage at a later date.

Upon reflection, the student decided that she wanted a predictable goal in her life, something that at times brought a sense of mastery, so she returned to complete her program. When she met her instructor in person for the first time at graduation, they hugged each other, and the teacher, seeing the fierce pride and joy of the graduating student, felt a renewed determination to support other students in deciding whether to continue in their degree programs.

As mentioned earlier, online students may more easily feel isolated, since they are not getting the immediate feedback that their onsite counterparts enjoy. Instructors who help students to succeed are the best online teachers, particularly for teaching the first courses in each program. When students stumble, these instructors often reach out to encourage them and inspire them to continue with renewed confidence.

In my experience at UOP, online students who take a break during their programs, a phenomenon known as *stopping out,* may never return to achieve their educational objectives. That is why instructors who truly believe in education wish to help their students overcome obstacles to educational success and attain the goal they set out to achieve, which is an undergraduate or graduate degree from UOP.

Distance education traditionally poses a particular challenge to student retention. Researching why online students leave is even more difficult, since locating out-of-attendance students and then getting accurate answers about why they left are challenging obstacles to valid research on this topic. Yet, from my discussions and reading, the following factors appear to contribute to online attrition:

- Students leave because of isolation.
- Students leave because of the accelerated pace.
- Students leave because of competing responsibilities.
- Students leave because of technical issues.

Isolation and Online Retention

When a student is alone at a terminal, no matter how many messages that student is seeing on the screen, he or she may still feel alone. Why? A student may find it more difficult to develop the same informal relationships in an online environment that arise onsite. However, mechanisms such as a student chat room and posting online biographies at the beginning of each class may help facilitate camaraderie and student bonding. Further, a student might miss seeing nonverbal communications from others. When a student feels stressed, he or she might pull back from the group more easily, since he or she will not "lose face" as openly as in an onsite classroom. This, in turn, may cause the sense of isolation to worsen.

The instructor should monitor all his or her students' participation and contact those who are not participating. Depending on the situation, a phone call may prove more timely and effective in reaching a student who appears to be nonresponsive to overtures from the instructor. Continued nonresponsiveness may demand that the instructor involve the university's staff, depending on the university's guidelines.

Accelerated Pace and Online Retention

Many online programs model the University of Phoenix's accelerated learning pace so adult learners can earn a bachelor's or master's degree while continuing to work full time. When the pace is grueling, students may leave for what they think is a few months' break, and then lose the momentum to return to school. Since students report that life never seems to slow down, the accelerated pace of an online program may be far more challenging than they initially anticipated.

Burnout is also possible, depending on whether a student can cope with the demanding pace of reading texts, discussing online, researching, writing lengthy papers, and completing study group projects. Particularly when time management is a challenge, students may procrastinate, being to accumulate "incomplete" grades, and then feel overwhelmed at the prospect of making up the uncompleted coursework.

Sharing time-management skills in the class, along with setting the evaluative criteria, providing regular encouragement, and giving clear feedback about students' progress will help keep students encouraged through long nights of studying at a distance. Occasionally, I have found it helps to focus the student on the pride he or she will feel on the day of graduation, and then move the discussion to his or her "to do" lists and small accomplishments.

Competing Responsibilities and Online Retention

Most students who choose an online program do so at least in part for the flexibility offered by a distance education program. Not having to be online at a specific time is attractive to busy working professionals. Some students, however, confuse flexibility with lack of rigor.

For whatever reason, it may be easy for a student to underestimate the commitment required to complete the challenging coursework of an accredited online program. This commitment often involves delaying gratification in other areas of life in order to succeed in the degree program. Turning on the computer after an exhausting day of work and family responsibilities may prove daunting, particularly if a student overestimated the time commitment involved in participating actively online as well as working on research papers and projects.

Even for students who knew what to expect when deciding to return to school, life might intervene and demand another analysis of school as a priority. For example, working adults are in the age range where they often face unanticipated work pressures (e.g., a downsizing or a promotion) as well as the dual demands of children and elderly parents. Any of these, particularly when a student is in an accelerated online program, may compete for attention with schoolwork and attainment of educational goals.

Students may consider withdrawing from a program due to feeling overwhelmed by work, home, or other responsibilities. Discussing with students the value of attaining their educational goals and helping them to prioritize will assist them in juggling their responsibilities while continuing to progress toward their educational objectives. Being flexible with deadlines is also an effective strategy. (For example, instructors often require that students must communicate with them before a deadline to arrange a postponement; those who do not do so are docked for lateness.)

Technical Issues and Online Retention

Occasionally, students encounter technical issues related to hardware, software, and their levels of proficiency with either. If the students are relatively nontechnical, the mystery involved in solving technical issues may seem overwhelming. Students may become so annoyed at their inability to set up an Internet service provider (ISP) connection, for example, that they get discouraged and frustrated instead of reaching out for technical assistance.

An online student prevented from logging on to the classroom is comparable to a onsite student driving up to an educational facility to find the doors locked. Being unable to reach an online classroom, for whatever reason, rates as an emergency that must be resolved quickly.

In the online classroom, issues related to software or hardware will likely arise. User issues can often be resolved by the online instructor or by other students in the class. Other issues may involve calling technical staff at the university or the software vendor. In emergencies, instructors often help students obtain the appropriate technical support, which is essential to the students' retention and success. For example, if the online university has a help desk that serves students and instructors with technical questions, calling the line for a student may help him or her receive more prompt attention and thereby decrease the probability of the student leaving the program.

Conclusion

Mastering the skills described in this chapter will bring online instructors the satisfaction of knowing that they can motivate, educate, and retain adult learners earning their university degrees through the online medium. With practice and commitment, they will be gratified to find that their efforts increasingly prove effective in producing the desired learning outcomes of the courses that they teach.

As educators expand and polish their teaching repertoires in the online medium, experienced online facilitators will help lead new instructors to adapt successfully to this flexible yet demanding and dynamic learning environment. As part of this adaptation, online instructors should build on the four areas of proficiency (visibility, feedback, materials, and retention) with fresh perspectives and innovative instructional strategies.

Reference

Kauffman, R. (1996, Summer). Assessing the virtual university. *Adult Assessment Forum,* 13–16.

7

MANAGING TIME

Developing Effective Online Organization

MARILYN SIMON

Time is a highly valuable resource. It is important that people spend it wisely. The adage that "by planning for the future, we can live in the present," long accepted in the business world, has profound implications in the academic world, especially in the online environment. Online teaching and learning require more independent facilitating and learning than onsite courses, and thus substantially more time-management skills.

Time management includes good program planning where resources (people and time) can be used effectively. Daily work is made easier when a model provides a continuing guide for action, various levels of accountability, and responsibility, and when essential tasks and sequences are specified along with a timeline for completion.

Both online learners and facilitators enter the learning environment with highly diverse life experiences. Life experience and prior educational experience have the greatest potential influence on learning. It is therefore critical that programs of study be designed to organize new information in relation to the learner's prior knowledge and learning style, and to integrate new knowledge with existing knowledge.

Some people think best in the morning, whereas others prefer the evening or afternoon. Online education presents the opportunity to maximize an individual's learning experience by selecting his or her own time to "be at school." It is important that the online student stays current with the work and asks questions to clarify any information that is unclear. However, online learning does not mean the student is totally self-supportive. It is critical to be able to connect with other learners, as well as faculty members, and to be aware of any online support services provided by the institution.

Online teaching is labor intensive. An online faculty member may be teaching two or three classes, taking part in a faculty-development workshop, mentoring another faculty member, and reading massive personal messages that require responses. How can he or she possibly make sense of all this information and still have time for a full-time job, a family, and a life? Understanding time and information management can substantially assist the online faculty member to improve learning outcomes and preserve that precious resource called *time*.

In the online classroom environment, all communication is written. There is a high expectation that the student will be sending several messages everyday and that the facilitator will be responding in kind. This is a complex situation that can become overwhelming and lead to burnout, or at least to a low desire to face the computer everyday. Effective time and information-management systems can be life preservers in this sea of information. This chapter will discuss ideas and methods that can assist members of the online learning community to improve time and information-management skills.

The Elements of Online Time Management

Many factors affect online time. First, the *subject-matter knowledge* a faculty member possesses is inversely related to the amount of time needed to respond to queries by students. It is unquestionably easier to compose a response if one is an expert in the area he or she is facilitating. A faculty member with little real experience in a subject area will essentially have to learn as the course progresses, and that can be quite time consuming. However, if a faculty member finds himself or herself lacking expertise in a course, or is a bit "rusty" in content knowledge, it would behoove the instructor to find a veteran faculty member to serve as a mentor. With permission, it would be wise to *lurk* in the mentor's online class. *Lurking* and *mentoring* are excellent means for any new online faculty to obtain the necessary online experience and to learn from a seasoned instructor.

Second, *keyboard skills* will largely determine time efficiency in a written communications environment until voice transcription technology becomes a more reliable alternative. Keyboard skills are a bottleneck anytime fingers on the keys cannot produce the written word as quickly as the mind can compose it. The goal here, as any good typist would say is to learn keyboarding well enough to compose words and even phrases in whole (i.e., typing without having to spell words out in one's mind at the same time). The good news is that the more one types, the better these skills become.

For years, the computer keyboard has been the dominant method by which words are converted from oral to written form. It seems a foregone conclusion that voice transcription will eventually emerge as the primary word-processing data-entry interface. Such technology already exists commercially and it is rapidly improving. Although embracing voice-transcription technology will require some short-term time investment, it promises to be a method that will improve long-term time-management skills. Those who will use word processing most productively in the future are likely those who have learned both excellent voice-transcription skills as well as excellent keyboarding skills.

Third, *software applications and skills*—the ability to identify and use reliable, effective software—can be a major time saver. This allows the user to cut and paste information and to move freely from one application to another. A database program that permits a faculty member to easily keep a record of individual student needs and work as well as student grades is an invaluable resource.

Fourth, a good *database-management strategy* can help the instructor focus on the unique information elements and the relationships between these elements. This means having information readily available on each student's academic work, needs, background, and interests in order to ascertain important information quickly. Taking the time to prepare a customized grade sheet template is a wise investment of time. It is critical that all assignments and correspondences are kept on file and that a copy of the syllabus be available whenever engaging in activities relating to the course. Keeping all this information in the same place, preferably by the computer, is a fundamental timesaving measure.

Fifth, *reading efficiently* is a must. Most online courses—besides being completely textual themselves—are accompanied by a textbook(s) and other supplemental printed and electronic materials. There are skills that one can employ to assist learners to be more proficient readers. For example, the learner should take time to reflect on what he or she is hoping to find before beginning the reading assignment. If there are chapter summaries or chapter introductions in a text, reading these first could elucidate the information. The learner should be encouraged to relate the information to something already familiar.

Regarding efficient readers, it is a good idea to become familiar with the common academic writing models of disciplines and authors. These include the following :

- *Cause and effect.* This takes place when the author explains a situation or theory and then delves into the consequences of its application. Cause and effect is prevalent in many sociology texts—for example, the author might describe the social learning theory and then describe a particular case that exemplifies this study.
- *Compare and contrast.* Here, the author examines two or more different theories or situations and their relationship to each other. Psychology texts that argue the Nature versus Nurture theory of child development often choose this type of presentation.
- *Process description.* In this case, a certain concept, program or project is delineated and then examples are provided. Many texts that discuss total quality management present information in this manner.
- *Sequential.* This is when a case is built in a linear or historical manner. Analytical texts frequently use this style—for example, in learning about linear programming, there is a step-by-step procedure that can be followed to obtain a solution.

It is extremely important that the online instructor help learners become active readers. This means asking questions such as: What is the author's purpose? Why am I reading this? What conclusion does the author come to? Do I agree with this?

Sixth, create a *working environment*. It is important that both the online facilitator and the online student create a place that is relatively serene and conducive for productive work. This special space should have the following luxuries:

- *Proper lighting.* Poor lighting increases eye fatigue. Ideal lighting is indirect and free from glare. Many people find fluorescent lights to be easy on the eyes and free from shadows.
- *Proper ventilation.* The brain needs fresh oxygen to function at its optimum. Weather permitting, keeping a window open would be an excellent way to satisfy this need.
- *Reasonable quietness.* Try experimenting with soft classical or jazz music in the background to see if that increases your concentration and productivity. Having Mozart or George Winston music at a barely audible pitch is believed to increase higher-order thinking skills such as creativity and critical reasoning.
- *Proper supplies.* There are basic supplies and tools that are necessary in one's working space, such as computer, modem, printer, textbook, syllabus, supplementary texts, clock, comfortable chair, telephone, surge protector, and a Do Not Disturb sign. When this sign is displayed, it must be respected by others in the household.

Time Management and Student Feedback

Trying to respond to each correspondence by each student could grind you into pine-nut powder. It is important to resist the temptation of responding to everything and saving all notes. Only selective responses are needed. Setting up a file for each student with essential correspondences can be a useful timesaving tool. Establishing a variety of meeting rooms and places to send correspondences is another organizing tool.

The facilitator sets the mood and climate for the learning environment. He or she should be brief but courteous. When responding, it would be best to quote the relevant passage, then highlight the message and add a response. *Cluttering* meetings with "I agree," "Me too," and "Thanks a lot" should be discouraged. This takes up a great deal of space and consumes valuable time. Constructive and pointed feedback is a time saver and helps cut down on the amount of communication. The facilitator should respond to personal questions within 24 hours if possible. A personal question could be an indication that a concept might need to be clarified for the entire class. A chat room where students and faculty engage in informal discussions helps free the rooms where the course information is explored, and helps save time on obtaining the type of information one is seeking.

Time Management and the Online Learning Curve

The learning curve effect is as real in the world of online teaching as it is anywhere else. If this is your first time teaching an online class, it is wise to start with no more than one class. Once you devise a study schedule and develop a routine, you will be able to add more classes to your online learning foundation.

On the first occasion, the time required to provide effective student feedback is always substantially more than the time it takes on the next occasion. Each subsequent feedback action requires less and less time. The same is true for the entire class facilitation process. Facilitating your first class effectively will require significantly more than it will take later on, as you gain experience. Each subsequent class requires less and less time. In part, this is due to having a database of lecture notes, supplementary materials, and templates that can be recycled and perfected over time. Although such time reductions are theoretically unlimited, it is a practical matter that the reductions, at some point, are no longer noticeable. Nevertheless, it takes many repetitions before improvements reach this point.

Decisions and Priorities

Managing time is a decision process. It is a set of decisions that recognizes time as a finite resource among tasks that are competing for this resource. An excellent first step in effective time and activity management is to write down your goals and the time you need to complete each one. Next, it is important that you recognize other things that you have to do, and want to do, during this time. Look over the list and put a 1 next to the most important thing you need to accomplish, and then number the other items relative to this list. Now break down each item into smaller chunks and make a weekly plan. First, fill in a calendar with all the time that you will be attending to your "have-to-dos." Next, fill in quality time that you can dedicate to your online courses. Choose something that you want to do that is not on the schedule, and plan for that as well. Remember that allowing time for family and friends are crucial in maintaining a fulfilling life.

Like many online professors, I wear several professional "hats." Besides facilitating online courses, I teach in traditional classroom settings in the evening, supervise research studies, conduct my own research and writing projects, and manage an educational consulting firm. I find that keeping an electronic calendar offers me the greatest flexibility and accessibility, and allows me to plan months, and even years, in advance. Printing out daily, weekly, and monthly schedules keeps me aware of current commitments.

I am a morning person. If possible, I try to do most, if not all, of my academic planning before noon, and then attend to my other professional responsibilities between 1:00 and 4:00 P.M. During a typical workday, I will be out of bed by 7:00 A.M., answer my personal e-mail messages before my first cup of coffee, complete some type of physical activity by 9:00 A.M., and then focus on my academic preparation. To set the mood, I turn on something like "December" by George Winston, and sign on to my online classroom.

Once online, I respond first to the most urgent messages in my personal mailbox. Once the fires are extinguished, I then check any assignments that are due on that day, and then move to the online classroom discussions. If a conversation is flowing smoothly, I will try to keep my two cents out of the discussion. However, if there appears to be a controversy or an impasse, then I will either offer my opinion or suggest means to seek a resolution. Once convinced that classes are flowing smoothly, I will then enter faculty discussions and bulletin boards. Usually 45 to 90 minutes is needed to accomplish these goals. The exception is on Thursday, when weekly grades are due. Generally, it takes 20 minutes per student for me to ascertain a weekly grade.

Effective time management is more than good technical skills. It requires appropriate priority decisions and flexibility. The time given to any task is the measure of its priority. Faculty members who devote 80 percent of their teaching time to the 20 percent of tasks and activities that really matter are the faculty members who are consistently successful in the classroom. Identifying "what matters" is the key to this process. Academic achievement is the objective when teaching. What constitutes the 20 percent that really matters when pursuing this goal in an online teaching or learning environment are issues directly related to student learning.

Time Management and Online Student Expectations

It is imperative to establish reasonable expectations and then fulfill them. The course syllabus and other curriculum materials will set the basic classroom expectations. This includes how many times a week a student is to be online, how often a student needs to respond to a discussion question, when assignments are due, and what must be accomplished to obtain a certain grade. From this basic set of expectations, a faculty member must explicitly consider how he or she can best assist students in fulfilling these expectations. It is imperative that students know how to obtain support, where they can locate information, how they are to deliver their assignments, and what the expected length of each assignment is. "Customers" are satisfied when expectations are met. A major element of the online instructor's job is to set appropriate expectations and then deliver the goods on time. Anything less will generate distractions from the primary academic achievement objectives.

A good syllabus serves as a scaffold for the course and clearly explains when assignments are due and how they are to be presented, as well as provides hints for how to manage time. A complete syllabus should be sent prior to the first day of class, and then weekly updates should be provided at the start of each week. Lowther, Stark, and Martens (1989) find that obvious items are often omitted in syllabi. The major content areas of a comprehensive online syllabus are course information (description and objectives), instructor information, text information (readings and materials), course calendar and schedule (due dates, exams, and special events), and course policies (attendance, participation, academic honesty, grading, and support services).

Following is an excerpt from an online course syllabus in quantitative analysis. Notice that the due date, the approximate length of each assignment, and what is expected of the student are delineated along with hints on how to manage time effectively.

1. *Reading Assignments*
   Read Chapters 4 & 5 in *Statistical Techniques in Business and Economics* and the corresponding chapters in the Study Guide. Each chapter is composed of four sections. You might wish to read two sections a day to stay current with the material and to allow yourself time for reflection. Keep a record of any concepts that you find confusing and need further clarification on. Post these to our main meeting room as needed.

2. *Chapter Assignments*
   Complete the Chapter Assignments found at the end of Chapters 4 & 5 in the Study Guide. Submit your assignment to my personal mailbox by Day 6. It might be useful to complete the material pertinent to each section as you complete that section.

3. *Quiz*
   Complete the Quiz provided on Chapters 1–3 (this is last week's reading) and submit this to my personal mailbox by Day 4. You might wish to do this before you begin delving into the new material.

4. *Application Paper*
   Last week you chose a topic you wish to research that is of professional or personal interest to you. This week you need to find a professional peer-reviewed journal in your field (or a field that you are aspiring to enter) and a lay journal such as *Newsweek* or *Time,* and locate research studies that use and abuse statistics related to your topic, which uses and abuses statistics. In week 3, I will send you specific guidelines on how to evaluate these studies. The studies you choose need to have a significant amount of numerical data, and at least one of them must have had a hypothesis that was tested using statistical hypothesis testing. Online journals are acceptable.

   If you have any difficulty locating such manuscripts, you might try conducting a web search or go to your local university library if possible. If this is not fruitful, please send a note regarding this matter to my personal mailbox. The completed paper is due at the end of Week 5, and should be between five and seven screens in length. Submit a brief update on your progress on locating these studies to our "application" meeting by Day 6.

5. *Discussion Questions*
   Please provide a brief response to the following questions and submit to our "main" meeting by Day 2. Respond to at least three submittals from others by Day 5.

Why do many people believe that "statistics is sadistic"?

How can knowledge of statistics change this belief?

6. *Weekly Summary*

Please prepare a weekly summary discussing the material you found beneficial this week. Submit your one- to two-screen response to the "summary" meeting by Day 7.

Time Management and Classroom Problems

Solving classroom problems can be very time consuming. Classroom problems are often the result of students who believe they are not receiving appropriate feedback or the result of some expectation that has not been met. As soon as a faculty member becomes aware of a classroom problem, it becomes his or her responsibility to deal with it. In the long run, it will save time if you give top priority to preventing classroom problems. Learning from past experiences helps prevent future problems.

A student with a negative attitude can drain energy and time from the class. The online facilitator must deal quickly with a student who is excessively contrary and appears to be dragging the class down. A phone call might be necessary to get to the root of the problem. In extreme cases, it might be beneficial to notify an academic advisor to encourage the student to reconsider his or her decision to take this course.

Preventing and Anticipating Technical Problems

The chief risk to electronic information is hard-disk failure. The most important risk-management strategy requires copies of the electronic information on separate storage media. Such storage media can include standard floppy disks, large capacity removable disk systems, zip drive, tape systems, external hard drives, network hard drives, or write or read CD-ROM drives. The more valuable the information, the more important the backup.

A hard-copy backup is the least technology dependent. This is an information strategy that is rapidly declining in use as computer power and computer skills increase. The hard-copy strategy essentially revolves around printed pages and some form of file-cabinet organizational techniques. Implementing this strategy is as simple as printing anything identified as potentially relevant for future use. The advantage of the hard-copy strategy is that printed information is not subject to the whims of computer hardware (e.g., hard-disk failure). Hard-copy information management strategies are also by far the least difficult to implement, requiring no more than printing or photocopying the desired data or documents.

One disadvantage of the hard-copy strategy is that printed information is retrieved manually. Unless great pains are taken to produce a functional index to the printed pages, then retrieval is often a matter of physically leafing through folders. Another disadvantage of this strategy is the need to reenter data when it is needed again in an online environment. It also kills trees.

Although hard copy is a low-risk information-management strategy, the future of this strategy seems doomed, as the restrictions of the hard-copy approach make it completely inefficient. Information proliferates rapidly in an online environment that forces online teachers and learners to use electronic information-management strategies.

A Final Thought about Time

Imagine that you had a bank that credits your account each morning with $86,400, and carries over no balance from day to day. Every night, it deletes whatever part of the balance you failed to use during that day. What would you do with such an account? Most likely you would make certain that you spent every cent every day.

Are you surprised to learn that you have such a bank? It's the TIME bank.

Every morning, the time bank credits you with 86,400 seconds. Every night, it writes off, as lost, whatever we have failed to spend or invest wisely. It will not carry over a balance. It does not allow for an overdraft. Each day it opens a new account in your name; each night, it erases your balance. If you fail to use the day's deposits wisely, the loss is profound. If you can invest about 10 percent of this resource each day, for your online courses, you will receive major dividends in your teaching and learning stock.

There is no drawing against the "tomorrow." No matter how wonderful your time-management skills are, you cannot get more than 86,400 seconds in a day. You must live each day on your daily deposit, and invest it wisely to get from it the utmost in health, happiness, and success from your personal and professional life! The clock is ticking. Make the most of each online day as well.

Reference

Lowther, M. A., Stark, J. S., & Martens, G. G. (1989). *Preparing Course Syllabi for Improved Communication*. Ann Arbor: University of Michigan, National Center for Research to Improve Postsecondary Teaching and Learning.

8

COOKING UP A SUCCESSFUL CLASS
Adapting Courses for the Online World

SHELIA PORTER

No longer is distance education the black sheep of the academic family, read about only in advertisements in the backs of magazines, with "courses" consisting of letters and red-marked assignments exchanged through the mail. In fact, online education today is one of the hottest topics in academic communities and corporate America. With the increased attention, more and more effort, study, and technology are being dedicated to making online education programs not only reputable but also a preferred method of education for some.

Online courses are courses delivered electronically by modem connection. At the University of Phoenix (UOP), online courses are highly interactive, even though students and instructors often sit many thousands of miles apart. I have facilitated courses for the Online Campus of the University of Phoenix since 1993, and derive many of my conclusions from that experience. I have also facilitated traditional onsite and distance courses for other institutions of higher learning, and therefore include observations from those experiences as well. In addition, I have trained and coached many of UOP's Online Campus faculty members and have discussed many of these topics with them in private and group meetings. Many professionals from other institutions have shared their experiences with me. I will synthesize those additional experiences along with other anecdotal information that I have gathered in my professional and personal studies in this area.

While many institutions are experimenting with video-conferencing, web-based courses, cable courses, and other methods of providing distance education, little information is publicly available about developing courses for interactive online delivery. In this chapter, I share what I have found to be the crucial ingredients of a productive and successful online course.

(Some of the inquiries that need to be made during the development of the courses may, at first glance, appear to be moot points, given the directives or resources of institutions developing or converting courses for online delivery. Yet I encourage all who are charged with such development to dare to challenge the existing paradigms when necessary. The process of determining what will work well in each specific online environment is analogous to the work of an experienced baker when moving from one climate to another. A basic cake recipe made in Florida at sea level with high humidity is very different from that same recipe in southwestern Colorado at a high altitude and very low humidity. For a truly delicious cake in both places, it is not a simple matter of mechanically changing the measurements. The baker must customize the adjustments of different ingredients and adjust the oven temperatures, baking time, and sometimes even the size of the pans to end up with a cake that rises well, looks good, and tastes great.)

Bandwagons are always popular to jump on, especially ones that appear to have huge profitability. Online programs are not for everyone, however, and will leave a very bad taste if poorly developed or delivered. As you have read in previous chapters, facilitating an online class well is not a simple matter of typing up lecture notes and making them available to students on a website. Similarly, developing an online class is not a simple matter of taking an existing class syllabus, typing it up, and requiring students to submit their answers to the instructor by e-mail.

This chapter provides the basic recipe to follow when developing an online class. Remember, though, you will need to customize the specific ingredients to create a course that looks and tastes great not only to you but also to the audience you will be serving.

One Part Course Content and Teaching Expertise

First, start with a cup of course design. Keep basic pedagogical principles, combined with real-life teaching experience, in mind. All UOP courses are developed by experts in their content areas, along with program managers who are conversant with accreditation requirements and sound pedagogical principles. The end product of the collaborative work is a written course guide called a *curriculum module*. Modules outline the objectives and assignments for each class session, recommend a grading scale, and provide faculty with suggested activities and assignment details to satisfy the objectives. Students receive an abbreviated module without the faculty notes. Individual faculty members create their own syllabi, which incorporate the modules' guidelines and provide all other necessary information such as details of assignments, deadlines, grading criteria, and overall course grade weight of assignments.

Most courses for the UOP Online Campus have been delivered first to students at one of the onsite campuses. In that way, the staff can see what has worked well in practice, not just in theory. The tried-and-true module from the onsite classes is then used as the basis, or starting point, for the online class. Adjustments are made by adding one part of this and other of that, to make it appropriate for the online environment.

For example, in a business law class I facilitate, students present oral analyses of adjudicated cases and current articles in the onsite classroom. In the online class, these same assignments exist, but students present a concise written analysis instead of an oral one, and then answer questions the other students and I submit to explain points of interest. Everyone is required to participate in the discussions at least five days of seven each week. The exchange is not quite the same as answering questions posed immediately after the speaker stops talking. But the result is a substantial amount of discussion by everyone who wants to discuss a specific case or article more. The discussion time is not limited by the agenda for the allocated class hour.

In both classrooms, my practice as a business attorney enables me to help students focus on the main concepts and laws they are likely to encounter in their work lives. My experience as a teacher enables me to understand how to communicate clearly with them without too much legalese, and figure out how to assess effectively their fulfillment of the learning objectives.

Some institutions have a more standardized approach for online education, disallowing individual faculty creativity in how the main topics of each lesson are presented. That is, some institutions provide the lecture materials and discussion questions each week (in the form of written materials or videos), limiting the faculty member's role to fielding questions and grading the work submitted. I have facilitated classes under both systems and have found the UOP Online Campus to be most satisfying for faculty and students. It is also most effective in terms of providing students with a personalized approach to what might otherwise be viewed as a program not far removed from the early days of correspondence courses.

Second, add a dash of an optimally sized class. The UOP program has determined that online classes function best when enrollment is between 9 and 13 students, due to the high degree of interaction between students and faculty on an almost daily basis. Conducting online classes with fewer students often results in too little discussion and expressions of fewer differing perspectives. Conducting classes with more students creates an unwieldy burden of having hundreds of e-mail notes to read and digest.

Third, blend in a half-cup of online classroom organization. When developing online classes, determine whether daily, weekly, or other periodic levels of interaction between students and faculty best meet the course objectives. For example, do you want a course in which all students read the posted lecture and assignment notes, then send their assignments to the instructor's personal e-mail box, or do you want the students to interact with each other? Or might a combination be best?

At the UOP Online Campus, each faculty member and student has a personal mailbox for private communications. Each class is designed with an open forum meeting that the faculty member and all enrolled students have access to throughout the course. Branch meetings, which instructors have the options to create, are typically used for the submission and discussion of specific assignments such as current article reviews, weekly summaries, and final course project papers. Discussions are held in the open meeting and branch meetings. Many assignments are submitted to these open meetings. Online students learn from each other as well as from the faculty member. Attendance and active participation are key components in the course design and grading criteria.

Many of the UOP online instructors organize their classes in the following way:

- *Main meeting.*   Students log in to this meeting on the first day of class and use it for the majority of their discussion notes about assignments.
- *Lecture hall.*   Faculty members post their syllabi, lecture notes, assignment notes, and other important notices in this read-only branch meeting. (The software prohibits anyone other than the faculty member from posting notes here.)
- *Article reviews.*   Many of the online classes include assignments to review and analyze current articles on topics raised in the textbooks.
- *Weekly summaries.*   Weekly summaries describing application of one or more of the main lessons learned are posted and discussed in this branch meeting.
- *Chat branch.*   Students and faculty use this optional branch meeting for noncourse-related topics

Fourth, add a cup of technological expertise—use "just the right amount of technology." Do not lose sight of the basic pedagogical principles when tempted by the technological lures to add pizzazz to the design and delivery mechanisms for courses. It can be very tempting to build in lots of video clips, for example, or graphics, but ask yourself whether they add to or detract from the focus of the course. How much time will students spend downloading and reviewing video or audio clips? Is that the best use of their time, particularly if the clips add little to the text or other written messages?

Similarly, what about the time students might spend adding to the font size and color of the text in their own messages, or even adding animation? Fancy fonts, colors and animation are fun and exciting, but if someone is pressed for time, I would rather have him or her spend it mastering the material rather than making the form of the message more fancy. Additionally, keep in mind that not all students have state-of-the-art equipment that can download large files quickly and store them all from a number of courses for a long period of time. Thus, the use of technology must balance with practicalities.

At times, however, the use of advanced technology is only wise. The adage *A picture paints a thousand words* is applicable here. In many situations, supplementing a narrative with a diagram or graph can help explain the message more clearly. Nevertheless, if you are going to ask students to use graphics in their assignments, consider whether they will need to dedicate inordinate amounts of time to the appearance of the assignment and the selection of the graphics. The result could be skimping on the content of the assignment. Be certain that everyone can view any graphics that you or the students create. Consider, too, the various hardware and software limitations. For example, users with Word 97 can read documents and graphics created with Word 95, but those with Word 95 cannot read documents created in Word 97. That seems like an obvious point, yet you would be surprised at how often faculty and students who have the latest version available might need to be reminded to use the lowest standard specified by the program.

In other words, clarify the objectives of not only assignment content but also assignment presentation as well as the design of the course. Keep those objectives in sight when writing the details of activities. Do not encourage the use of advanced technological features if their use will substantially detract from time dedicated to the content of the course.

Choosing the Best Software

Online educators today have numerous software options. Software will continue to evolve, and because it would be inappropriate to mention only a few by name, I will outline here the characteristics that have proved to be not only "must haves" but those that are greatly advantageous as well. You can make your own educated choices based on what is available when you are ready to develop your online courses.

"Must have" features for software include (1) it must be affordable, easily installed, and easy to learn basic features such as reading, writing and sending notes; (2) it must run well on affordable computers (i.e., ones that most students and faculty are likely to have, generally not the latest, fastest, fanciest computers on the market); (3) it must have the ability to move and export notes singly or in groups; and (4) it must have the ability to create branch meetings off the main classroom for specific assignments and discussions.

"Nice to have" features include (1) both offline and online readers; (2) built-in viewer to allow users to read attachments in various formats, such as PowerPoint, Excel, Word Documents, and so on; (3) different size and color fonts, as well as features such as underlining, bold, and italics for text; (4) the ability to sort notes by sender and subject; and (5) the ability to embed hyperlinks into lectures and other notes to allow easy access to Internet sites.

Regardless of the software used, my experiences in conducting online classes and training faculty have convinced me that irrespective of the level of computer-user sophistication, students and faculty alike experience many frustrations when left totally on their own to learn the specific program software. Consequently, some orientation to your software needs to be provided to students as well as faculty to help them be successful in the classroom. Additionally, training for faculty in online facilitation skills will help greatly.

Video and Audio Supplements

Some institutions use only text formats for distance learning class activities. Others do not yet use the Internet or computers at all; they rely on mail, cable broadcasts, or videos of lectures, accompanied by texts and workbooks, along with written assignments that are mailed to instructors for grading. One institution where I served for a short time as an adjunct faculty member used a video and mail-in assignment system along with university-sponsored private voice mailboxes for faculty and students. Faculty members sent in at least one voice message a week to the class voice mailbox and students called in with specific private-message answers to assignments. These voice interchanges provided the individual touch and interaction that the standardized video approach lacked. That system, however, did not provide the high degree of interaction and effectiveness that the UOP Online Campus system provides.

Although there is no voice component in UOP online classes, there is always the option of calling each other on the phone, as necessary, to clarify something instantly or to defuse a situation that needs immediate attention. Additionally, some of the online class modules are accompanied by videos that students purchase to supplement the text. Still others utilize texts supported by websites that provide updates and supplemental activities. So remember, combinations of technologies can work well, and recommendations (or even requirements) for their use can be built into the curriculum to honor different learning styles.

One Part Financial Expertise

In this part of the recipe, begin with a cup of financial investment in the design. Seriously consider the financial costs of design. Could teams of developers working together develop the course best? For example, the basic objectives, lecture areas, and assignments could be outlined by a content expert—someone who has successfully taught the class in a traditional classroom. It would also be best to have that same person, or a codeveloper, be experienced in a facilitative style of online teaching. As you have already read, simply providing a typed lecture for the online classroom does not work well. The instructor needs to pose questions that stimulate thought and that promote lateral learning. In the online classroom, even more than in the face-to-face classroom, the instructor is most effective when she or he is the "guide on the side" rather than the "sage on the stage."

Second, add a pinch of someone who understands the abilities and limits of the method of delivery. Such a person can provide incredibly valuable assistance at the course development stage. After all, it would be disastrous to give assignments that require students to submit charts or graphs if the software will not allow the transmission of them. On the other hand, if all assignments are limited to written reports, but the software allows the transmission and viewing of PowerPoint or other presentation software slides, you would be unduly limiting the creativity of submissions if you did not allow that method of assignment completion without good reasons.

Third, throw in a tablespoon of financial costs of equipment and software for the school, instructors, and students. The major cost of computer equipment for an online education program may not be borne by the institution providing the program. The classrooms exist in cyberspace, so there are development costs for the class and for the server or Internet service that collects and redistributes all the electronic messages created by the instructors and students. However, the traditional areas of cost savings to the school are great because there is no real estate to be bought and no real property taxes to be paid for the classrooms.

This does not mean the classrooms are totally free for everyone. Unless you are going to be the extremely rare institution that provides computers to all faculty and students and that pays their telephone and Internet connection costs, there are faculty and student costs in the form of computers, Internet service provider accounts, and telephone lines, though some of this can be reimbursed. Although your institution may be able to afford whatever computer equipment it needs for the support staff and administration, not all students or instructors will be able to write checks for unlimited amounts. So, keep these costs in mind as you develop courses.

Also keep in mind the costs of connection and specific course software. Will you be providing it free to students, or will there be an extra charge for it? Next, you need to know what other software is compatible or will cause conflicts while operating. For example, one of today's popular distance educational software is incredibly memory hungry and will give you messages saying your computer is "out of memory." You need to find either a different software or let users know that such messages may occasionally appear. Provide instructors as well as students with information about what to do (other than panic) when they see such messages on their screens.

Develop a profile of the minimal, basic configurations of computer equipment necessary. For example, let students and faculty members know about recommended or required computer speed, memory, graphics capabilities, CD-ROM or floppy disk drives, speakers for audio files, modem speed, and the dial-in option chosen (direct modem or Internet service provider). Additionally, consider how you will assist students and faculty in gaining proficiency with the connection software. Will they learn it from manuals? Will your institution provide a web-based tutorial? What technical support will you provide?

Finally, make it clear to faculty and students that faculty members are expected to provide technical support to the students. The UOP Online Campus has an entry course for undergraduates that combines readings and discussions about skills necessary for beginning college degree studies as well as how to master use of UOP software. Although students are strongly encouraged to take advantage of a technical orientation, not all do. Faculty members in beginning courses need to provide software assistance; the course is written to allow for a sharp learning curve in the first two weeks. Later courses, however, can safely jump right into the contents of the course on the first day.

One Part E-Mail Communication and Writing Expertise

Messages, of course, are conveyed by much more than the words themselves. For example, if I write to a student, "I can't believe you wrote that in response to my last question," that message would most likely be read very differently from, "I can't believe you wrote that in response to my last question. :-)"

In the former instance, the student might be concerned that I did not agree with or approve of what she or he had written. In the latter example, however, the student would have a visual clue that I was OK with what was written. I am not ordinarily a "smiley face" type person, but I have found that using a few selected emoticons in the online classroom is helpful. Online instructors need to come across as complete people, not just the ones making assignments and grading them. Emoticons help create a relaxed environment at appropriate times. By the same token, when I have a serious message to deliver, such as, "I haven't received your assignment that was due yesterday; please contact me ASAP," I don't want to inappropriately insert a smiley face even if I am tempted to convey a friendly tone. In other words, developers should know that it is imperative when designing online courses that someone needs to be assigned to work with faculty to help them understand the ways in which they can often supplement online messages.

In addition, online *tone* is important. Experienced users of e-mail messages are often fans of brevity. A brief, to-the-point note can be read much differently than it was intended, however. For example, if I am concerned about how a student is doing and about whether I have received all assignments, the following note to the student is assured to elicit a different, more negative reaction than the second one:

> Bill, I don't have your completed assignments that were due yesterday. Send me proof you sent them in on time, or let this note serve as your notice you have earned an F for them.

Wouldn't you rather receive the following:

> Bill, I don't have your completed assignments that were due yesterday. Perhaps I inadvertently overlooked them, or they didn't yet make it to the right meeting? Please let me know when you sent them in, and if you don't see them in the main class meeting, please resend them ASAP and let me know what happened. Of course, if you didn't send them in before today, please let me know that too and then send them in ASAP to obtain at least partial credit for them. (Please see the syllabus for partial credit for late assignments.)

Giving the student the benefit of the doubt, acknowledging when there might have been a misunderstanding, asking for clarification instead of making assumptions, and allowing him to save face form the foundation of proper online tone. A *please* here and there often help, too. Although these suggestions may be commonsense options for some, they are not in the forefront of the consciousness of many online developers and instructors, especially when writing e-mail messages. If there is not going to be specific training about these communication skills for faculty and for students, some coverage of them in the modules and other course materials may help keep instructors on the right track and working productively together.

It may not be fair to expect perfection in every single message sent to every single mailbox, but it is reasonable to incorporate standards for written communications. The module or syllabus should clearly state the expectations of writing perfection in the daily class notes. Of course, it should go without saying that the modules should be free of typos and other grammatical errors, as well. Remind faculty to proofread their own syllabi, lectures, and other notes to practice what they teach in all daily messages.

One Part Accreditation Expertise

I mentioned this part of the recipe briefly at the beginning of this chapter, so I will just briefly reemphasize it here. It helps to have someone on the development team at least review the proposed course design and compare it with the requirements of the appropriate accrediting body. The last thing you want is to have a course ready to deliver, only to determine later that it is missing an important element or is deficient in a required area.

Begin with a dash of legal expertise and beware of both sides of the copyright coin. Of course, no one wants to turn course development into a complex legal matter. Nevertheless, some basic information about important intellectual property issues may save you a great deal of time, energy, and money later. There are many other legal issues that may be relevant. Nothing in this section should be construed as legal advice, so, as in any situation, if you have specific legal questions or concerns, do consult an attorney. You may want to consider the following issues:

- *Clarify ownership of the course.* Always have a written agreement between the people actually developing the course and the institution for which it is being developed. It should state who owns the course as well as other crucial terms such as amount and timing of payment for the development. A common myth is that the author of a creative work always has the right to use the work or to copy it. The law, however, distinguishes between the rights of an author and those of the copyright owner when a work is created for another. The safest practice is to put the express agreement in writing, so the intentions are understood from the very start.

- *Honor others' copyrighted material.* One of the unfortunate by-products of access to computers and familiarity with the Internet is that it is easy, and, for some, tempting, to copy materials created by others. In the United States, in general, the creator (or employer of the creator when the works are "works for hire") automatically owns the copyright to original works "fixed in a tangible medium," even when there is no notice of copyright shown on the work. So, when in doubt, assume that copyright laws protect work created by someone else. That means it is not legally permissible to copy pages or parts of pages from the Internet or other sources. Institutions need to make it clear that those who are developing courses for them are to be the authors of original work they provide to the institution, or, if they are not the authors, they are to provide written permission to copy from the copyright owner. (There are "fair use" exceptions to the copyright laws, but these must be carefully examined on a case-by-case basis for materials one is going to use under this provision of the law. Chances are that for repeated use in a course, the fair use exceptions will not protect the institution.) Developers and faculty need to know that not only can institutions be held liable for copyright infringement but the individuals causing the institution to use the infringing materials can also be held liable under federal civil laws. In just the right circumstances, criminal prosecutions can result, as well.

And a Cup of Marketing Expertise

What good is a course if no one knows you offer it and if no one understands it is a part of a "real" degree program? Despite the fact that I spend the majority of each weekday in an online environment, I regularly talk to people who have no idea what we do at the Online Campus and who question whether it is as good as traditional education. Marketing the program consists not only of efforts to sell it, to obtain students, but to educate others about the program, as well. Marketing professionals can best market what they understand and have personally experienced. Consider providing them with information or a firsthand look at how an online class operates in practice, not just in theory.

Not only can marketing professionals help promote your courses but they can also provide the developers with information about what potential students are looking for and expecting. Use their information when you design courses. They may help lead the content and teaching experts in an exciting direction. The overall efforts of marketing experts are an integral part of the recipe.

Conclusion

As you can see, the good news is that you can develop interactive educational courses utilizing current technologies for delivery; the bad news is that it is not as simple as typing up existing class materials. Developing or adapting a great online course is not an impossible task, however, if you have the right ingredients.

9

GETTING READY

The Syllabus and Other Online Indispensables

MARILYN FULLMER-UMARI

The online classroom addresses the concern made by that Oxford University's business school dean, Douglas Hague, regarding business schools for not "delivering education that meets the needs of changing times, i.e., instantly available, instantly tailorable to increasingly divergent student needs." This chapter will examine the role of the syllabus and lecture as the foundation to fulfill the mission on high-quality online instruction.

As an online instructor, I frequently receive questions about this method of instruction. Among the most frequently asked questions from faculty, friends, and colleagues who hear about online are the following:

- Does an online syllabus differ from a traditional syllabus? How?
- What are the necessary elements of an online syllabus?
- How does an instructor gain and maintain high levels of attention and involvement from students who are reading an electronic lecture in the absence of gestures, animation, and other visual cues?
- How do you illustrate instructional points in the absence of traditional classroom visual aids?
- How does an instructor decide how long a lecture should be?
- How, in the absence of visual cues, does an instructor understand if a student comprehends the lecture?
- Are there any pitfalls that I should avoid in preparing my online lecture?

Preparing the Online Syllabus

The syllabus establishes the course guidelines and is the basis for a successful learning experience. The first contact that the online student will have with the instructor is the online syllabus. Through the syllabus, students receive class information about the instructor, course learning objectives and topics, the schedule of reading and written assignments, and information about course expectations and policies. Several factors are of particular importance for the design of your course syllabus:

1. *Class size.* An online class of adult learners presents a wonderful opportunity for sharing by classmates and subsequent horizontal learning. Variations in class size, however, will directly influence requirements for participation, use of branch meetings (see Chapter 8), and note management. In the onsite class, a larger class size requires effective facilitation to promote a balanced discussion among a greater number of students. As the number of students in an online class increases, the same expectations of participation will result in a proportionately higher number of notes for students to read and assimilate. This can become overwhelming and detract from a well-paced class environment.

In addition to reducing the number of days that students are required to participate in the class, expectations regarding maximum note length should be clarified at the outset as class size increases. Students should also be instructed to download notes more frequently in larger classes to stay caught up with the class discussion. Finally, establishing branch meetings for the instructor's lectures, homework, and noncourse-related conversation becomes more important in larger classes. For example, I create a meeting that I call the "Class Lounge" to facilitate my ability to maintain a focused discussion of course topics in the classroom while not discouraging the students' needs to socialize and build relationships. The influence of class size on these aspects of the online classroom can be addressed as modifications to the syllabus.

2. *Technology.* The technology available to your online students creates important considerations for your scheduling of assignments. You should take advantage of the learning opportunity presented by this technology for both the timing of reports and projects as well as provide a well-sequenced schedule of increasingly challenging assignments. The instructor's syllabus should reflect a sequence of assignments that will give students sufficient time to learn the online methods. The level of student competencies in data acquisition and use of electronic tools will vary broadly. Moving too quickly into technologically complex requirements

can result in students needing to spend excessive time learning the technology and thus less time in preparing the actual project.

Appropriate integration of technology into class assignments can assist students in learning the skills that apply to the workplace. Course requirements, when used effectively, will support students' workplace performance. The starting point for designing assignments is to assess what level of skills students really need. As one student commented to me at the end of our class, "While I was reluctant at first to try using media that I was unfamiliar with for my assignments, the requirements for the final course project forced me to explore new methods and has made me a more valuable contributor at work now in the preparation of reports and presentations."

The syllabus for students taking their first online class will need to anticipate and address the higher level of uncertainty that students experience as they begin working in the online classroom. The focus in the first course should be on mastery of the technology used in the online program. Courses should introduce students to the Internet and the Web, acquaint them with resources that are relevant to the course, explain how to conduct searches, and, depending on the technology of the course, instruct students to develop their own personal webpages. For courses early in the program sequence, I instruct students to research and submit a list of 10 resources that can be used as references for future work in our class. This assignment allows me to assess the students' familiarity with the information environment available to them on the Net and the Web. A systematic approach to integrating technology into your courses will enable you and your students to utilize available tools effectively rather than being overwhelmed by them. Based on your specifications, students will submit assignments that may include spreadsheets, audio and video attachments, pictures, and other electronic learning aids. It will be important for you to have clearly identified objectives for using these tools so that their inclusion does not become entertainment focused.

3. *Class sequence and course length.* The syllabus should present a schedule of the readings and assignments distributed over the course to allow adequate time to cover each area. Match readings and class assignments to support learning objectives. Keep in mind that online education is already a reading-intensive medium, so you may want to reduce reading assignments slightly in comparison to the onsite classroom. For entry-level students, it will be especially important to have all assignment requirements clearly outlined in the syllabus.

4. *Well-designed course objectives.* Two purposes of the online course will be to convey information and knowledge and to create a learning experience pertinent to the subject at hand. The instructor must do this through the selection of assignments appropriate to adult learners and the online medium. The selection of each assignment should not only support course objectives but also recognize the strengths and limitations of the online classroom and the preference of adults to take responsibility for their learning experience. For example, while adults value horizontal learning that study groups provide, the online medium must take into account time zones and turnaround time required for asynchronous discussions and assignment preparation.

5. *Degree of course flexibility.*   Many online students are attracted to distance learning programs because they cannot be in an onsite classroom each week due to travel or other schedule conflicts. The appeal to online students of being released from the requirement to be in a classroom at a certain time and place on a regular schedule should be kept in mind regarding due dates for assignments.

In preparing the course syllabus, instructors should evaluate how important it will be to the mission of high-quality instruction in their online classes that students submit assignments on a specific due date. To best meet the needs of many online students, it is desirable to offer some flexibility. I do this whenever possible by providing target due dates but also allowing additional time to submit assignments without penalty.

6. *Setting the tone.*   In the onsite classroom, the instructor's appearance, voice, and comments can help establish the tone for the course. Similarly, online instructors use their syllabi to set the tone for their virtual classrooms. Decide on the degree of formality/informality that you want for the class and present your expectations in your syllabus regarding classroom climate. This can be accomplished by including the instructor's availability online and offline to assist the student, evidence of some flexibility and willingness to work with students, expectations for a professional tone and conduct in the class, as well as a demonstration of the instructor's willingness to be open. This sharing can begin by including brief biographical sketches at the opening section of the syllabus. As one student offered: "My experience so far is that most instructors are very open about themselves and their past experiences. This helps in providing a trusting and supporting environment where the people in the class can get to know each other and thus are able to more effectively communicate as a class."

Elements of an Effective Syllabus

This section presents a list of essential elements that are required for an online syllabus. While some requirements are obviously more important than others are, this list provides a solid foundation for the outline of your course.

1. *Course description and overview.*   The course description and overview provides an introduction to the subjects that will be examined in the course. As students read this over, they are looking to see not only what will be covered but also which topics will stimulate their interest. This section is an opportunity to get students really connected to the class. Will the course description communicate the importance and relevance of the ideas to be covered to the students lives? The instructor who understands adult learners and their needs will create a description that connects the course topics to the competency-based needs of adult learners. The well-designed online course overview will generate energy and promote student commitment to the course subject and medium.

2. *Instructor biographical sketch.*   This will be your students' first look at who you are. The nature of your course will determine what your students will want to know about you. I use a slightly different biographical sketch for different courses so that I can share relevant academic and professional experiences without becoming too detailed. I also personalize my biography by sharing some of my interests and hobbies. I try to communicate information about myself that lets students know that I value an environment of open communication where students can feel free to share their opinions. I include some humor to show that humor is welcome, as well, in my class. I also share a story that models a willingness to take risks and to be open to new experiences. Most importantly, I try to demonstrate that I am committed to the possibility of each student in the class having an incredible learning experience as well as being a partner in our learning adventure. Many faculty refer students to their own personal webpages where students can "see" their instructors.

3. *Instructor contact information.*   The majority of student contact will come through the online meetings and e-mail. I communicate to students that I care about them and I make myself available to them by providing the best times to reach me offline by phone. I state clearly that they can expect to have all questions or telephone calls returned within 24 hours.

4. *Schedule of readings and assignments.*   Your syllabus should include the reading and written assignments for each week of the course. This schedule allows students to anticipate their workload and plan ahead for potential time conflicts, thus enabling them to keep pace with the class. Your schedule should recognize holidays and the potential travel and additional time demands associated with these events. Although a student may be able to do an individual paper during a holiday weekend, it may be difficult for study group members to coordinate their schedules to complete a joint project.

5. *Review of class policies.*   You may want to cover the following items when discussing your class policies:

a. *Attendance.*   Present either the school's general attendance policy or your own expectations regarding how attendance will be taken online and the policy regarding absences. For example, attendance may be counted as logging on at least once during the class week. If the student does not log on during that period, an absence is recorded. The syllabus should state the number of allowed absences in a class and the affect, if any, on the student's grade.

b. *Grading.* The syllabus should include a clear statement of the grading policy and the timing of instructor feedback. Provide an outline of the requirements for each assignment and the relative weighting of points. You might also consider including a statement regarding how grade disputes will be handled.

c. *Participation.*   The policy regarding participation requirements is a critical aspect of the syllabus. Your policy should emphasize both the importance of participation to the learning experience as well as how participation will contribute toward the student's grade. My participation policy states both the level of activity that I am looking for in terms of frequency of participation as well as makes suggestions for contributions. Here is a sample of an online policy on participation:

Class, I want you to know that I'm going to facilitate our discussions in a way that I hope will make this an outstanding learning experience. I'll share my own views and examples. I'll offer questions about your comments. I'll try to generate mini-debates so that we really examine these issues from different perspectives. I invite you to question me, challenge me, and certainly don't hesitate to disagree with me.

   If your favorite topic or question doesn't come up, please take responsibility for generating a discussion on that. If you want me to address a topic that I haven't covered, simply ask the question. This is your class. You can help generate the learning experience that you want by your own involvement. Each of you has a valuable contribution to make. Don't wait for the topic to come up or be asked to share an example. Jump in. The more involved you are and the more you take ownership in our class, the richer the learning experience will be for you.

Also, we could talk about any subject each week, but I encourage you to stay with our planned sequence and rigorously discuss and examine the material that is the focus for a given week. You will find that the continuity that this focus creates will open possibilities for higher-quality discussion. In terms of grading your participation, I'll be looking for substantive and insightful examination of our week's topics on five of the seven days each week. A total of five points can be earned for each day of participation.

d. *Tone in the classroom.*   The comments from my students again and again refer to how much they enjoy and learn from our class discussions. The level of activity and the quality of the participation will determine the quality of the class. The syllabus can set expectations for a respectful and professional tone in comments and feedback. I also encourage students to avoid sarcasm, since the inherent negative effect of sarcasm is amplified in the online medium.

e. *Late assignments.*   You need to decide how you will handle the submission of late assignments and state that in the syllabus. Will late assignments be accepted? If so, will there be any penalty in the form of reduced points for late assignments? How will due dates be adjusted for students in different time zones? Will late papers from students who experience system difficulties also be treated as late in terms of penalties?

f. *Exams.*   Many onsite instructors give students "take-home" exams. Similarly, online students can complete exams at home and submit them at a specified time to their instructors. Some schools may require a proctored exam for a midterm or final, whereas other schools may permit all exams to be taken online. The syllabus should include your policy and schedule for exams, so that students have time to plan for taking the test. When I use exams in my online classes, I assign brief case studies that require students to apply course concepts in an analysis of the problems presented. I then can allow students to use their texts.

g. *Academic dishonesty.*   With some online resources making course papers available to students for a small fee or free, the problem of academic dishonesty is always present. The syllabus should present a clear policy regarding the seriousness of plagiarism, the forms of plagiarism, and the consequences for students in terms of course grade and academic status. The following is the policy of the University of Phoenix regarding plagiarism taken from the *Online Faculty Handbook:*

All the work submitted by a student must represent the student's original endeavor. Where outside sources are used as references, work submitted by the student should identify the source and make clear the extent to which the source has been used. Ideas or work presented in the private or public forums of the online electronic classroom are subject to the same standards of honesty. The University considers plagiarism and falsification of documents, including documents submitted to the University for other than academic work, a serious matter that may result in the following sanctions:

1. Failing grade for the assignment and/or course.
2. Suspension from the University for a specified period of time.
3. Permanent separation.

6. *Request for student biographical sketches.* In the onsite classroom, students typically introduce themselves during the first meeting of the class. The introductions are kept brief due to the time constraint on the meeting. With online, students have the opportunity to send more descriptive biographical sketches. This ability to have a detailed sharing of one's experience and career history is another advantage of the online format. In the onsite classroom, this level of detail in personal history and work would be prohibitive to share, since it would be very time consuming. These more complete biographical sketches in the online class can be valuable for the students in getting to know one another and building a class bond as well as seeing the wonderful diversity of experience, perspectives, and work affiliations.

    These biographical sketches can be sent to a separate meeting so that students can review them at their leisure. Because of the absence of visual cues, online students tend to be very interested in reading each other's biographies. This will also be very helpful to the instructor when making an assessment of class learning needs in preparation of lectures and other course materials.

7. *System information, formatting, and note and file management.* A brief section in the syllabus should be devoted to frequently asked questions as well as system difficulties. Also, if you have preferences regarding limits on student notes to the class, file sizes, or the formatting of notes, state this in the syllabus. For example, you may choose to instruct students to excerpt briefly a portion of the note or lecture topic that they are responding to and to use subject headings on comments to the class. This section can also clarify your expectations regarding length of assignments (in terms of the online equivalent of a page) and suggestions for students to follow regarding management of files, including saving all course homework until the final course grade has been received.

Preparing the Online Lecture

Just as the concept of the library with its rows of books and quiet cubicles has changed to include online collections of digital articles and texts, the online classroom is forcing a reassessment of the definition of the lecture. The lecture as an instructional method has been subjected to increasing debate and criticism, particularly in regard to its appropriateness for adult learners. Much of the disfavor associated with lectures is that, by its very nature, the lecture puts students in a passive role while the instructor remains at the center of attention. The next section of this chapter will examine the role of the lecture in the online medium.

Redefinition of the Lecture

The key to understanding the new possibilities presented in the online lecture will be clearer after distinguishing the environments of the online and onsite classrooms. An understanding of the characteristics of the online environment can enable the online instructor to assess and implement effective techniques to create an exemplary learning experience:

1. *Diversity.* The online classroom can be distinguished from the onsite classroom by the opportunity it offers for greater differences in the composition of the class. When people think of diversity in the onsite classroom, the focus is more on differences in class composition based on gender, race, physical or learning disability, status, socioeconomic, and/or professional status. In contrast, these dimensions of diversity are generally not apparent in the online class. Instead, the online class can be made up of students from around the country or world who would never otherwise be able to assemble together for onsite instruction. This diversity poses a challenge to the instructor to develop a lecture (or lecturette) to meet the needs of a potentially wider range of students in background, experience, and expertise.

2. *Absence of time pressure for delivery.* When an instructor walks into the onsite classroom, he or she is aware of time management responsibilities and the need to deliver his or her lecture, review and collect homework assignments, answer questions, and leave adequate time for case discussions, class presentations, and so on. The clock presents a physical reminder and scorekeeper of the instructor's efforts to manage his or her class effectively. Requests to clarify project requirements, questions about the reading, and even the insightful question about course material can

end up competing with the time allotted to the lecture. How many onsite lectures have been concluded with, "We are out of time, so read the rest of the chapter, and we'll try to get to any questions that you have on it next week"? The well-prepared lecture material on this unpresented section of the text is closed in the instructor's notebook and, with the time limit, the class misses out on the complete presentation of the lecture. In the onsite classroom, these factors influence the amount of time that the instructor gives to a lecture as he or she balances varied demands and determines which ones should receive priority for the course period.

The benefits of the absence of a time limit on the online lecture presentation is evident in the comments from students, such as the following:

> In the traditional classroom, the teacher and students have the allotted time available. With the online lecture, if material is complex, you can take a break and then continue with a fresh mind at a later stage. In the traditional classroom, you have to digest the lecture when it is served. This makes the online experience much more rich than the traditional lecture experience.
>
> I think the online format allows the student to analyze the material at a rate that is more comfortable. With the onsite lectures, the ability to comprehend the subject matter is hampered because of time constraints.

In the absence of a time constraint for the online lecture, how should online instructors decide on the lecture length for their presentations? Some instructors take into consideration the nature of the course itself in determining the length and structure of the lecture. For example, lectures in graduate and qualitative courses are somewhat longer than undergraduate and quantitative courses. Many online instructors design a series of mini-lectures to send out over the class week. I prefer the use of mini-lectures that include questions to stimulate discussion on the material. The exception to this is that for courses early in the program sequence, I send out all of the lecture material at the beginning of the week so that less-experienced students can see the overall scope of our discussions, thereby giving them more time to pace their studies.

Finally, online instructors recognize that the medium requires students to do a great amount of reading and therefore most keep their lectures to about 1,500 to 1,800 words. Many students say that an online lecture, unlike the onsite lecture, can never be too long and students need not be embarrassed in class for "dozing off." As one student comments: "The lecture is as long or as short as the student's attention span. The student can continue or stop at will." The online environment provides students with the opportunity to truly manage their learning experience.

3. *Distractions in the onsite and online class.* Two examples will be discussed here—the environment and the instructor:

   a. *The environment.*   As an onsite instructor, I always looked forward to presenting lecture material that I had worked on to provide a stimulating and rich learning experience. My preparations and delivery in pursuit of the "flawless lecture" sometimes competed with holding the attention of students distracted by late-arriving classmates, postdinner dullness, and preoccupations with families or jobs that had been left in order to spend the evening in class. For some students, there was the problem of late evening fade-out. I may have been well prepared for the lecture, but the students' mental readiness and the presence of classroom distractions were not fully under my control.

Distractions in the online environment also exist for the online student who is attending to a lecture. However, the feedback that I receive from my online students suggests that they utilize their ability to manage their study time to control distractions, as these comments illustrate:

> In the onsite lecture, I often found myself missing bits and pieces of the lecture as I attempted to get the main points into my notebook after a long day at work when I was tired. Onsite lectures are also, unfortunately, affected by peripheral considerations that can relate to the physical facility in which the lecture takes place, including temperature, seat comfort, those sitting nearby, and so on. With the online lecture, none of these peripheral considerations is relevant. There are no facial expressions by the instructor to guide the student's thought one way or another. I can choose the setting and time for reading the lecture. My practice is to review it when I am mentally alert. If I choose, I can read it first thing in the morning, and I can review it several times during the week. I can read it over the first time to get the main idea and then again carefully to cull out the main points. I can even cut and paste the lecture into any format I feel comfortable with. With the traditional lecture, when students are overly tired, there is a tendency to "zone"; unfortunately, they cannot then go to bed and catch it again in the morning when they are fresh. The online lecture gives us that ability.
>
> It is a challenge to juggle professional, family, and school responsibilities while also trying to find time for any leisure activities. I tend to live with my portable PC, and consequently, I find myself doing schoolwork whenever there's an opportunity. Lately, I have spent a lot of time at airports and on planes, and I will often use this time to read through lectures and other related reading materials. Usually this works fine, but for some

work you need peace and quiet. For lectures, I usually get up early before the family is awake.

Online instructors can minimize distractions by writing lectures in a very readable format, presenting full text within a clearly outlined framework. I make my lectures more readable by alternating several different strategies within my presentation of material. These breaks in "pace"—such as designing a lecture that includes mini-cases, presenting opposing viewpoints on a subject, debriefing course material, applying course concepts to my own professional experiences, and asking questions that challenge students to examine course topics rigorously—create a "living" lecture, the purpose of which is to stimulate my students to be involved critically and creatively in the conversation.

b. *The instructor.*   The quality of the onsite lecture depends on my own delivery and the many factors that will influence that outcome. For example, either my own energy level or the grade dispute that I received moments before I left for class can affect my concentration and thus adversely impact the quality of my delivery of the lecture. In addition, my physical appearance or speaking voice may be a distraction to students, preventing them from becoming more attentive to my otherwise well-crafted lecture.

In the online lecture, visual cues and similar causes of inattention do not exist. In contrast to the onsite lecture, the content and delivery of the online lecture are student focused and become an interactive discussion between the instructor and the student. The online instructor redirects the student to learn new material, amplify and relate course concepts to current professional experiences, and thus become a true partner in the design of the learning experience. In the online lecture, when instructors upload their lectures to the class, each one can potentially deliver that "flawless lecture," irrespective of a long day on a consulting project or a temporary case of laryngitis.

4. *Nonverbal cues.*   Many instructors enjoy the performance aspect of delivering the onsite classroom lecture. Some may enjoy dazzling the class with the drama of the presentation of the historical crisis, using theatrics to make a point. Is there some dramatic equivalent that can be drawn upon in the electronic lecture? Does this drama help promote a student's learning? The following student comments offer evidence that the excitement of the onsite lecture is a real part of the online lecture, as well:

Sure, I have had some charismatic onsite lecturers, but I think that the most charismatic ones have been the online ones ;-) really! In a traditional classroom setting, the students are "forced" to absorb the lecture within a given time period and without any breaks. Consequently, the students will often fall into mental lapses throughout the lectures, and the lecturer therefore needs to build some "drama" into the lectures in order to keep the audience awake. This is not the case for online learning where the student can pick the time for studying and can also take breaks or go back and reread parts of the lecture. Nevertheless, there are many ways for the online lecturer to prove charismatic and add some "drama." I think that humor is the most important tool for this.

Quite frankly, I prefer the lack of distracting "drama" from the instructor. Good novelists can write such artifices into their books; so can online instructors.

Purposes of the Online Lecture

The development of an exemplary online lecture will take into account both the unique environment and opportunities of online education as well as the purposes of the lectures and the implications for the role of the online instructor.

Provide Motivation

Given the competency-based orientation of adult learners, it is very important that the online lecture be aligned to the learning preferences of adults. While mastery of the subject material is a primary objective of the lecture, the lecture can also contribute to the learner's motivation to master the subject material. Once instructors have the biographical sketches of their students, they can design the lecture to include material that will appeal to the learning interests of their students.

I stimulate student interest by inserting brief examples or "mini-cases" into my lecture that apply course concepts to the students' specific industries and problems. By facilitating this linkage of course concepts to students' organizational experiences, students become motivated in this learning process. As one student told me, "I look for an understanding of the material that has been integrated into real life or practical examples, and a discussion on the application of the material." This motivation of students to examine real-world application is amplified when the examples discussed are relevant to their own workplaces and experience.

Organize and Prioritize Course Material

The lecture helps to organize and prioritize the material for the week, but the *effective* lecture will do this in a way that involves the student in this process of framing the subject at hand. Rather than writing a lecture that gives solutions and best practices, the lecture can be used as a compass that allows students to select their own direction and to question and apply course material to their own experiences and observations. Instead of presenting material as "answers," the lecture can invite students to evaluate the material and raise new questions. The lecture can instruct students to take on a specific workplace problem, examine it in terms of course material, and report their findings to the class as part of their participation for the week. For example, course material on organizational structure can be the basis for the student's evaluation of the appropriateness of their own organizations' structural designs.

Function as a Technology Conduit

Given the vast resources available to students online, the instructor is in the role of reducing a large amount of information into a manageable number of topics and resources. Online instructors will find themselves "enablers of learning" by acting as a conduit to varied resources based on the learners' needs and interests. The lecture can instruct students to research additional reading material or applications of the topics for the week and to share these resources with the class.

Provide a Model

The instructor's openness and willingness to take some risk through the sharing of professional successes and mistakes can provide a model to students. Online instructors can model other behaviors that are expected in the classroom, such as using a positive and professional tone, making encouraging comments to students, using humor, and critically examining the material.

Stimulate Critical and Creative Thinking

Use well-placed questions at appropriate points throughout the lecture to invite the students to judge, assess, apply, refute, and underscore the impact of what is being accomplished in the presentation. In the onsite classroom, where instructors often feel pressed for time and must move forward through the material to be presented that day, students are not allowed much time to reflect on questions, and so the potential of this technique may not be fully realized.

In contrast, when the instructor raises an insightful question in the online lecture, students can be invited to take a few minutes to reflect on this, to critique the idea from different viewpoints, to think about how a technique can be used in their own organizations or to suggest a solution to the problem. The lecture may be ended with an "electronic field trip"— an invitation to the students to visit a relevant Internet site. For example, the instructor of a psychology course could send students to an Internet site where they can take a temperament-type test.

Provide a Referral Base for Future Study and Questions

Links embedded in the lecture can break up material with referrals for additional study on the material at hand. Business students can be referred or linked to Internet sites that give examples of the business model that was just discussed. A music instructor could refer students to Internet sites to compare the music of Mozart and Beethoven. Depending on the technology of the students, these electronic sidebars can be made optional or specific requirements for the course. The instructor must be aware of changing or unreliable Internet links and select those known for stability. It is a good idea to routinely verify the viability of the links by asking students to indicate any links that are not accessible.

Steps in Developing an Online Lecture

1. *Capture and maintain interest.*   The efficiency of an online lecture saved to a computer file is obvious. One need only retrieve the file and the lecture for the week. But the ongoing improvement and transformation of your online lecture is a process that will make your role as an instructor more interesting and stimulating. If you want to make learning exciting to students, you must continue to find teaching itself exciting and challenging. With the ability to modify, update, and adapt each lecture to the unique class composition at hand and against a backdrop of changing events, the core lecture can be transformed for each new class. Biographical sketches submitted by students at the beginning of the class can provide the basis for an assessment regarding modification of learning objectives and lectures that are customized to the composition and needs of the group.

In addition, you will want to identify ways to establish rapport with students who are about to take in the lecture. Onsite instructors can establish rapport with a glance, smile, or gesture, or even by walking among the class members. In contrast, online instructors will convey enthusiasm for the course with the language of the lecture, humor, the sharing of personal and professional examples, and "delivery" style. I have had numerous students tell me that the energy and personality of an online instructor can be effectively communicated "right through the screen."

2. *Develop the individual lecture.*   The lecture will operate on three levels: First, the online lecture efficiently conveys information, theory, and subject knowledge to the student. In the absence of real world examples, this level basically offers the student a general formula to apply to the common situation.

The lecture moves to a second level with your questions about the theory and concepts covered and the presentation of problems that require students to sort out background facts and issues, apply course material, and develop logical alternative courses of action. You may further stimulate students' thinking by adding the third layer, which challenges them to test the ideas or techniques discussed—for example, by examining the relationships among specific concepts, applying material to their organizations, comparing conflicting points of view, or identifying problems, constraints, or exceptions.

The difficulty level of the lecture content will typically change over the course, because with each week, the students are developing and becoming more experienced learners. Thus, the elements that are used in the first week's lecture cannot become a firm template for the entire course.

3. *Prepare the mini-lecture.*   The onsite class lecture is commonly oriented to the average student in the class in terms of learning interests and background understanding. Questions from students who need additional help or from students motivated to discuss more complex topics are handled before or after class and on class break. You can use the mini-lecture to offer comments to meet the specific needs of these two student groups.

Think of the lecture in terms of two components: the core or primary lecture, which is offered on the first day of the class week, and the mini-lecture which is offered as needed on different days over the course. The mini-lecture, is a 600- to 800-word lecture that can be used to target additional comments on specific subjects or to reach smaller interest groups within the class. It may happen, for example, that the text focuses on large organizations but the class has several students who are small-business owners. In this case, the instructor may want to supplement the primary lecture with mini-lectures that address these learning interests and the concerns relevant to small business owners.

If the class is composed of a cluster of students in one profession or from one industry, such as telecommunications, you can develop a mini-lecture that applies general course material—for example, on managing change—to examples that reflect changes that are taking place in the field of telecommunications. The benefits of the targeted mini-lecture are evidenced in this student's observation:

> I have loved the willingness of faculty to offer extra insights in mini-lectures. In my finance class, the text left me baffled, but I found the extra insight from the instructor's targeted lecture extremely helpful.

Conclusion

The online environment offers the exciting possibility for instructors to redefine the nature of the course syllabus and lecture from the traditional teacher-oriented approach to one where the online student becomes actively involved in the learning process. Online instructors can use their syllabi and lectures to engage adult learners in a mental conversation that encourages them to question prior assumptions and that challenges their thinking about strategies and current organizational practices. The online syllabus and lecture offer the possibility of a dialogue, an alliance between the instructor and student as partners in the online learning process.

10

ONLINE FACILITATION
Individual and Group Possibilities

PATRICIA ADDESSO

Few things have changed business, education, and society as much as the explosive growth of electronic communication. More and more, one hears of virtual teams in the workplace, virtual classrooms in universities, and virtual relationships in both business and social contexts. Many professionals are beginning to rethink their basic training and skill base, including medical technicians, psychotherapists, and trainers. The world of the instructor must change, as well. How can instructors translate their skills in a way that is useful to the new age of online communication?

It is not difficult to access information these days. Anyone with Internet access has a wide variety of information available to him or her. A traditional teacher who simply provides information can almost be superfluous. But a facilitator is someone who makes learning possible—a role that is even more important today. This chapter will discuss the art and practice of facilitating learning in the online environment.

Before beginning, a few definitions must be clarified. The *facilitative method* refers to a partnership in which the faculty and students join together to meet learning objectives. The knowledge that each student brings to the classroom is just as important as the knowledge the facilitator brings, and each student learns from fellow students as a result of the facilitated learning discussions. Such facilitation presupposes interactive, group-based learning. The discussion is not about correspondence courses or other one-way teaching methods, nor is the discussion about one-on-one relationships with an instructor.

This chapter refers to learning that is conducted in *asynchronous* fashion. That is to say, students and faculty are not on their computers at the same time, and there is no resemblance to a chat room. People using chat rooms converse in "real time." They are all on their computers at the same time, and any message sent by any of the participants in the conversation is seen almost instantaneously. In a message board or news group, a note is posted for all to see. Then the board is checked once or twice a day, to see new notes, responses to the original posting, and so on. That is what is meant by *asynchronous*. The facilitator, for example, will post a reading assignment, some comments, and a discussion question or two. The students can read the materials, think about the discussion question, and respond. They then engage each other in debate, agreement, or argument about the topic(s).

In the sections that follow, I will look at the ways in which online facilitation is similar to traditional facilitation. I will then explore a model of online facilitation, including how to break the ice, how to use specific facilitation skills, and how to deal with common problems.

Common Ground: Traditional and Online Facilitation

Facilitating learning in classroom or work groups has a time-honored tradition of basic and advanced skills. Contrary to many people's first impressions, there are many transferable skills between traditional and online facilitation. In fact, in some ways, facilitation is more effective online.

Consider the many techniques facilitators have developed to deal with the participant who monopolizes the conversation. In an online discussion, no one is able to speak louder, take up all the "air time," or dominate due to physical characteristics such as height or attractiveness. Although paying attention to the process is still important, facilitators in the online environment have more opportunity to concentrate on ideas and knowledge.

Traditionally, facilitators also have to pay attention to the preconceived notions he or she brings to the classroom. In the online environment, it is not possible to judge a participant on regional accent, race, ethnicity, or style of dress. This is a huge plus for many people who may not have been "heard" in previous groups due to such differences. Not only the facilitator but also all the participants have a "purer" sense of each other, as it is unsullied by those preconceived notions.

In the asynchronous environment, there is a distinct separation between *listening* and *talking*. Students "listen" by downloading everything that has been "said" since the last time they logged on. They read the "conversation," paying attention to the pieces that interest them the most. They can then go back over the conversation, pick out the pieces they wish to respond to, and do so. There are no lost opportunities to speak, no sense that "I didn't get a turn." In fact, each student may be required to participate as a part of the grade. This process makes it much easier to listen, question, and clarify.

The traditional guidelines on facilitation take on fresh life when applied to the new world of online education. In his book *Freedom to Learn,* Carl Rogers (1969) lists the following nine Guidelines for Facilitation. Let's look at each in turn and see how it applies to the online environment.

1. *"The facilitator is largely responsible for setting the initial mood or climate of the program."*

This is as true online as in the traditional classroom. The facilitator's initial introduction to the course sets the tone as well as the response to each student. For example, an instructor's introduction may include both professional as well as personal information, as shown in the following excerpt:

> I have a Ph.D. in Industrial Psychology and I am currently an independent consultant operating out of San Diego. My work includes. . . . On the personal side, I have lived in San Diego all my life (tough job, but someone has to do it!). I have an office in my home where I spend about 60% of my time. I have an 18-year-old cat and a 15-month-old, 17-pound Pomeranian dog.

The instructor may choose the same friendly, casual tone when responding to introductory notes from students. (*Note below:* "Carat" marks > indicate a quote from a previous note. Also, correspondence examples in this chapter contain fictitious student and company names.) Consider this example:

> ------In note #35, Joe Smythe wrote:
>
> > I am a Purchasing Manager for a company called Acme. I work at the corporate headquarters in Dallas, Texas, and live in a great housing development right near downtown.
>
> >I am single, but engaged to be married to my girlfriend Judith in September.

-----Patricia Addesso replies:

Welcome! We will look forward to your input.
What kind of business is Acme in?
I get to Dallas a couple of times a year on business--I enjoy the downtown area also, but it's been a little too hot this year!
Congratulations on your engagement!

2. *"The facilitator helps to elicit and clarify the purposes of the individuals in the class as well as the more general purposes of the group."*

Clarifying purposes takes place from the initial communication in the online course introduction and syllabus (see Chapter 9). Then each individual can express his or her expectations of the course. The question, "What do you hope to gain from this course?" can be answered as part of each student's biographical introductory note.

3. *"The facilitator relies upon the desire of each student to implement those purposes which have meaning to him or her as the motivational force behind significant learning."*

Assignments, reports, and discussions can revolve around implementing the students' goals. If the goal is to apply the course content to the job, for example, online students can be asked specific questions about how a concept or theory applies in the real world.

4. *"The facilitator endeavors to organize and make easily available the widest possible range of resources for learning."*

The online environment is a great spot for implementing this guideline. At the time he wrote these words, Rogers could not possibly have imagined the resources at one's fingertips in the Internet environment. The key here is to make the resources available and leave the responsibility in the hands of the students.

When I occasionally ask students to look up an article. Some students will ask, "Well, where do I go? How do I find it? Can't you just FAX me the article?" Providing this student with the article does provide her with a resource. But giving some tips on finding it provides a richer resource that can be used again and again. (Remember the adage: "If you give a man a fish, he will eat for one day; if you teach him to fish, he may eat for a lifetime.")

5. *"The facilitator regards himself or herself as a flexible resource to be utilized by the group."*

The art of facilitation is best summed up by the word *flexible*. A facilitator knows when to let a conversation go, when to step in and redirect, and when to wrap it up and introduce another topic. A facilitator also decides if and when to interject opinions or facts into the discussion.

Although the time frames are different, the techniques are the same online. In a classroom, a facilitator may have to wrap up a discussion in 20 minutes, so as to move on to the next agenda item. Even if the class is a smaller, seminar-type group, chances are that not everyone has had a chance to articulate his or her views.

The same online discussion may take several days. In the course of that time, each student may have answered the initial discussion question, responded to classmates' notes, and participated in a lively debate. The facilitator decides when to introduce another topic, often simply by observing the tempo of the discussion and noting when it is getting circular or seeming to reach a natural conclusion. The facilitator also chooses the time to introduce his or her own perspective. If, for example, there are a couple of points that he or she considers vital, and those points have not been brought out, the facilitator may interject them. This process is also not all that different from what happens in the traditional classroom.

6. *"As the classroom climate becomes established, the facilitator is increasingly able to become a participant learner, a member of the group, expressing his or her views as an individual."*

Similar to the Guideline 5, this one has to do with interjections on the part of the facilitator. The traditional teacher role makes it difficult to express opinions, as most students are used to taking the teacher's opinions as "law." Communication skills such as coping with uncertainty, labeling opinions as such, and seeking disagreement are very helpful. For example:

------Note from Patricia Addesso:

I think getting employee input into decisions is a critical part of a manager's job. I imagine there are times when it is not appropriate, though. What do you all think?

7. *"The facilitator takes the initiative in sharing himself or herself with the group—feelings as well as thoughts—in ways which neither demand nor impose, but represent simply a personal sharing which the student may take or leave."*

As with Guideline 6, this one requires a certain tentativeness of communication as well as a willingness to expose oneself as a human being. For example:

----Note from Patricia Addesso:

I can certainly remember my first supervisory job. I was 19 and made supervisor of the night shift at a supermarket. I felt amazingly confident, as I look back now. I realize today that I was woefully unprepared both personally and by the organization. My staff included much older specialists in their fields, such as the butchers back in the meat department who would not dream of respecting a 19-year-old female college student. It didn't occur to me to be concerned!

8. *"Throughout the course, the facilitator remains alert to expressions indicative of deep or strong feelings."*

Deep and strong feelings are present in the online environment, just often a bit subtle and sometimes difficult to "read." A long post from someone who is ordinarily succinct may indicate a strong feeling about something. A "disappearance"—a student who is ordinarily quite participative being quiet all of a sudden—may indicate deep feelings, as well. Of course, it can also mean that the person got busy at work. The sense that something is going on needs to be even more carefully clarified online with the absence of other cues.

In a recent class, we had a discussion on personal values and how they affect decisions. For the first time (four weeks into the class), we discovered that we had an African American military man in the class, an Asian, and a lesbian. The resultant discussion on personal values became quite heated, with the military man telling the lesbian that he was sick of hearing about her homosexuality. Handling such an incident in the traditional classroom would probably have been far more disruptive to the group than this was (see Chapter 12). We all learned something from it, though: What is "right" and "wrong" is subjective, and all of us can be tolerant and accepting right up until our own personal values are challenged.

9. *"The facilitator endeavors to recognize and accept his or her own limitations as a facilitator of learning."*

As a facilitator, I am not the expert or the final word on a given subject. I can say things like, "That's interesting! I never thought about it that way before." I can assign cofacilitators to small group breakout sessions. I can do any number of things that are actually quite freeing; I am under no obligation to have the right answer or to be the ultimate authority.

The preceding examples show that, even though Rogers could not have imagined the online environment as it exists today, his guidelines for effective facilitation still hold up quite well. With these guidelines as our base, the next section will look at a model for online facilitation.

A Model of Online Facilitation

Breaking the Ice

To begin a class, the faculty member may send an introduction of himself or herself as well as the course, and a comprehensive syllabus to the class mailbox. Each student may be instructed to send an introduction and brief biography, as well, including information on how much exposure each has had to the topic of the class. For example:

> Hi all!
>
> My name is Elizabeth Grey and I am in my sixth class here. I see a lot of familiar names from Accounting—aren't you glad that's over?
>
> For those of you I haven't met, I am a Director of Human Resources for a small company called Futura. We are located in Atlanta, Georgia, and I live about 20 miles south of Atlanta in a small community called Elmsville. I have a wonderful husband, two kids (one of each gender), and an OLD OLD cat (she was seventeen last month).
>
> I'm looking forward to a change of pace this class. I have been in a lot of the quantitative-type courses (Statistics, then Accounting) and Organizational Behavior looks like a breath of fresh air, from what I have seen of the materials.

Each student and instructor should also have a personal mailbox. That allows for interactions that are inappropriate for sharing—for example, assignments turned in, grades or progress reports, and some constructive criticisms.

Facilitation Skills

Basic facilitation skills include such things as demonstrating an open and accepting attitude, listening to understand, and responding to clarify. Let's look at how each of these three skills translates to the online environment:

- Demonstrating an open and accepting attitude in traditional classroom may be done through maintaining eye contact, nodding, moving away from the podium or table, dressing appropriately, and paying attention to gestures. None of these are possible online. So how do you demonstrate an open and accepting attitude? Techniques like the use of open questions, use of students' names, reinforcement, and encouragement also demonstrate an open and accepting attitude, and all of these possibilities can take place online. For example:

  What have the rest of you experienced in regard to this issue?

  Jennifer, excellent example, thanks!

- Online facilitators must listen in order to understand the meaning behind student comments. In the online environment, the words used are extremely critical, since the nonverbals cannot be seen. One must always ask, never assume (which is a good rule of thumb under any circumstances.) For example:

Joe, that last comment about the incident at work sounded a little angry. Were you upset at your boss when you wrote that note?

Often, the student's private mailbox is used for such feedback. For example:

Joe, your last exchange with Maria in the class mailbox sounded a bit sarcastic. I don't know if you meant it that way, but maybe saying something like "I think we can look at it this way" instead of "It is clearly obvious to anyone who is paying attention . . . " would come across better. Thanks!

- Online facilitators often respond to clarify meanings. This is done through silence, allowing the speaker enough time to clarify his or her comments, or through summarizing and paraphrasing, and then checking for agreement.

Sometimes when an online facilitator sees a "strange" comment in the mailbox, silence for a time is helpful. When the student sees his or her own note, he or she will sometimes append a revision, saying something to the effect of "Whoops! That came out wrong." Or a fellow student will ask a clarifying question.

Otherwise, the techniques are the same as those in a traditional classroom. Instead of paraphrasing, the instructor can copy the part of the note that needs clarification, then ask the question. For example:

Re: Note #357 from Russell Jones

>I disagree. I have never seen this in my 25 years as a manager.

------Reply from Patricia Addesso:

Hi Russell,
So you have not experienced this phenomenon. Interesting. Why do you think that is? Remind me, how many different companies have you worked for?

Some of the more advanced facilitation skills also work very well online with just a little revision. Some of the skills include connecting ideas to experience, integrating materials over time, empowering and motivating others, and maintaining a group learning environment. These skills do not require face-to-face interaction, since they are more oriented to communication skills in general.

Let's take the advanced facilitation skills just mentioned and look at some examples of their use in an online situation. Questions are excellent ways to facilitate adult learning (Bateman, 1990). The following are actual examples of discussion questions used in a master's-level organizational behavior course:

- *Connecting ideas to experience.*

     Discussion question: Tell us about a time that you tried to change someone else's behavior at work. What did you do? Did it work? What could you have done differently, using the text or lecture material as a guide?

- *Integrating materials over time.*

     Discussion question: What connections do you see between Margaret's example and the discussion we had last week about cultural diversity in teams?

- *Empowering and motivating others.*

     Discussion question: Thanks for all of the great examples of high-performing teams you have been on. Would anyone care to take a shot at summarizing some of the commonalties between the examples?

- *Maintaining a group learning environment.*

     Discussion question: Your small group assignment this week is to discuss the case study on pp. 435–437. Identify issues related to organizational behavior that appear in the assigned case study, then analyze the issue using the theory from the text or outside research. Identify which of the areas on the model on p. 29 of the textbook the issue fits. (For example, is there a communication problem, a motivation problem, or ... ? How do you know?)

     The optimum value will be received from this assignment if you spend much of your energy discussing and analyzing the organizational behavior issue.

     My hope is that you spend a lot of time in the small group meetings just helping each other understand the issues.

Common Problems

Some of the problems familiar to facilitators are students who are noncontributors, monopolizers, distracters, and know-it-alls. These problems pertain to onsite as well as online classes. Many of the familiar techniques for dealing with them only need to be revised a bit for online, and in fact can work even more effectively. For example, handling a monopolizer in a classroom often means telling him or her, "I'd like someone else to address this question first." Online, that communication can take place in the student's private mailbox, saving him or her from possible embarrassment:

> *Sharon, I appreciate your enthusiasm and your detailed responses to the discussion questions. My concern is that your classmates are sometimes left with very little to add! Please delay your response a bit, so that others have a chance to think about it. Thanks.*

This problem becomes additionally complicated when the person is a quality contributor. One particular woman in a class of mine had a tendency to take over discussions and assignments. Far from appreciating it, her classmates resented it. In a private conversation, I likened her behavior to a manager who does not delegate. Since the degree she was pursuing was in management, it was easy to draw some conclusions about how she could use the classroom environment to hone her management and delegation skills, instead of doing all the work herself.

For the noncontributor (who may just be an introvert), "calling" on them in the classroom is sometimes counterproductive. He or she might easily become embarrassed and tongue-tied. A personal note online may say:

> *George, you made only two comments to the main class discussion all last week. Is there a problem or something keeping you busy elsewhere? We'd like to hear more from you this week. Remember, 25% of your grade in this class is based on your participation in the discussion and case study analyses.*

Introverts are often more outgoing in the online environment, simply because they have more opportunities to think about their responses and do not have to wait until their turn to talk. Those that are simply less active, however, do need some encouragement. I have had students who felt somehow less qualified to comment on a situation than the others in the class. "I'm just an administrative assistant," said one student. "These other people all seem to have lots of management experience!" Again, the techniques for handling this do not differ at all from what would be done in the traditional classroom. Tell this student how valuable his perspective is, and reinforce contributions with a "Good point, John!"

Distracters are familiar to traditional facilitators, as well. They may take the discussion off track, talk about irrelevant issues, or otherwise disrupt the flow of the class. This, too, can again be handled through private online communication. Another technique is to create a separate mailbox for socializing, referred to by some online facilitators as the *break room,* the *hallway,* or the *student lounge.* Those students who wish to socialize can do so and those who do not may choose not to "enter" the room.

By now, it should be clear that the last common problem mentioned earlier, know-it-alls, are handled by way of personal communications and working to diminish the impact on the class. A know-it-all may be sent a message similar to that sent to the monopolizer.

The first time I was preparing to teach a class online, I got a call from one of the students ("Frank") about a week before the class started. Frank introduced himself, we chatted a bit, then he proceeded to tell me all about another student who was a problem. "We don't like Joe," he said. "He's a know-it-all and hard to get along with. Can you make sure to keep me and my friend Nancy out of any group assignments with Joe?"

Frank and I chatted a bit more, as I checked the roster. Frank's address showed that he was from a mid-sized town in the South, as was his friend Nancy. Joe was from New York City. I decided that I would not take on the responsibility for keeping the feuding parties apart, but would attempt to facilitate a solution.

"Joe has a bad temper," said Frank.

"What did he say or do that led you to conclude that?" I asked.

"We were working on a small group project and Nancy and I had talked about how we wanted to work it. When we told him about it, he got mad and said we obviously didn't care about his input."

"What other interpretations can you think of for his reaction?" I asked. It took some digging, but Frank eventually saw that perhaps Joe was hurt, felt left out, or had even had a bad day at work.

Some issues are specific to the online environment. (Or are they?) Let's look at two that are commonly mentioned: the "How do I know it is really him?" question and the inability to see nonverbal behavior.

One of the first things many instructors who are unfamiliar with online teaching say is, "How do you know your student is who he says he is?" That question, of course, applies in the traditional classroom, as well. Few instructors check identification. In large lecture-type courses, for instance, a student could send a friend in on mid-term day. It is difficult to explain, but people do have online personalities. Without consciously tracking it, an online instructor becomes familiar with a student's tone, word use, and other characteristics. In fact, it is easier to see when a paper may not be a student's original work because every interaction you have with a student is written.

What about the issue of not being able to see nonverbal behavior? First of all, interpretation of nonverbal behavior is often wrong. Thus, in some cases, there may be actually less misinterpretation online. Second, online communication has developed a series of emotional indicators (called *emoticons*) to indicate humor, sarcasm, astonishment, and so on. As an example, if someone makes a statement that is meant to be humorous, he or she will often type in a colon, a dash and a right parentheses. :-) Looked at sideways, this forms a smiley face. It is somewhat simplistic, but effective.

Conclusion

If you have ever facilitated learning in a classroom or a boardroom, you already have some of the skills to do so online. The basic guidelines for facilitation, as laid out by Carl Rogers many years ago, provide a fertile common ground for providing the link between traditional and online facilitation. Think of the facilitation process in three parts: (1) the importance of breaking the ice in a positive way, (2) the use of all of the basic and advanced facilitation skills that you have available to you, and (3) the knowledge that problems can be handled and solved. When you break the process down this way, it is clear that there is no mystery about effective online facilitation. The time has come for this new and effective way of teaching and learning.

It is difficult to imagine the changes that will take place in a few short years when it comes to online facilitation. Whether talking about educational institutions, organizational training, or meeting facilitation, everyone must be prepared to face changes in the way they do business. The critical point here is not to say, "It can't be done," or "It can't be done well," or even "It shouldn't be done." The point is to hone your own skills so that when you are asked to facilitate online, you can transfer your current skills effectively.

References

Bateman, W. (1990). *Open to Question.* San Francisco: Jossey-Bass.

Rogers, C. R. (1969). *Freedom to Learn.* Columbus, OH: Merrill.

11

KEEPING IT FUN AND RELEVANT
Using Active Online Learning

AL BADGER

Any form of active learning that is fun or relevant to a student's professional or personal life tends to motivate the student more than just a lecture on or discussion about the subject matter. If learning can be made interesting, then students will learn more. Although online instructors are eager to get students started on online activities, their successful application requires coordination and time-management techniques unique to the online environment. This chapter will demonstrate, through a discussion of asynchronicity, pacing, and the instructor's role, how active learning can be successfully incorporated in an online course. Sample lesson plans will follow each of the topics of discussion to provide examples of the concepts presented.

The Application of Online Activities

Instructors who use active learning often justify their actions with reference to the motivation they provide students. Active learning tends to motivate students. Many educators would agree that if learning can be made interesting, students will learn more.

Not too surprisingly, the same philosophy concerning active learning holds true for online classroom activities. In fact, the online medium is a natural active learning environment, as it continues to attract and motivate people who seek information via asynchronous online discussions, game playing, and information searches. The advent and continued popularity of Newsgroups, ListServes, and Internet gaming zones are only a few examples of how the medium has become an untamed information source and learning environment for millions. Given that active learning tends to thrive in the online environment, it would seem the natural choice for many instructors in online education to choose the pedagogy of active learning to get the point across to students.

This is not to say that conducting online class activities is easy. To help explore these techniques and minimize this challenge, I will explore barriers to successful online activities and then demonstrate how active learning can be successfully incorporated in an online course by considering asynchronicity, pacing, and the instructor's role.

How the Asynchronous Nature of Online Affects Online Activities

I am not to ashamed to say that when I first heard the word *asynchronous,* I had to pretend that I understood what it meant. Peers and colleagues would bandy the word about in online discussions while I just pretended to understand so I didn't look too stupid. For a while, I thought it might have been a new type of modem or a new teaching technique. After a short time of working online, though, it was not too hard to figure out what people were discussing. They were discussing the time modality used in an online class.

The asynchronous nature of online learning means that the students and instructor need not be at one place at one time to participate in the class activity. Think of learning in an asynchronous mode as a glorified e-mail system in which you have personal and group mailboxes. At some time during the day, you log on to your Internet account and mail just appears in these boxes. The mail could have been sent at any time of the day and is just waiting for you to log on to download it. Hence, it is unnecessary for you to log on to the Internet at the same time the sender does. Through experimentation and application, this method of exchanging ideas has evolved and become the heart and soul of asynchronous communication and learning within many educational institutions.

The difference between public and private mailboxes rests in the number of people who can read the mail. For example, it is in the group mailbox where all the public notes are sent and the main spot where the class takes place. At the University of Phoenix Online Campus, the public mailboxes are used as classrooms for discussion. Anyone who sends a message to a class mailbox is sending it to a place for all to see and respond to. This format has many advantages and some disadvantages.

The upside is that asynchronous learning networks eliminate the instructional impediments of space and time while providing a degree of student-faculty interaction and collaboration that is truly unique. Schedules become flexible. No one needs to wait for others before attending a class. Students from different parts of the world can participate in the same discussion. One student may be in New York and another in China, and they need not wait for a specific time and date to respond to a note in a public mailbox. Rhythms of communication are established within a few days. Discussions and exchanges of knowledge begin to flow, class rapport is established, and responses are allowed considerable time for reflection before sent. The class comes to life as the students and the instructor are involved.

Of course, the asynchronous mode has a downside, which is mostly related to the delay in response time. When students and the instructor ask a question or respond to each other, they often have to wait a full day to get a response. When you add to this mix of 8 to 13 students in one class who are sending and responding to each other, waiting for a response to a message, a comment, or a question could be as long as two days. This time delay can be problematic when it comes to running group activities, for just getting 13 people in an asynchronous mode to discuss and agree on a concept could take a week. Some of the activities that I have conducted in a standard classroom do not last more than an hour or an hour and a half. However, in an asynchronous online setting, that same activity can take as long as a week to complete. Hence, when dealing with a delayed response time, remember to gauge the length of the activity carefully.

Now that I have exposed the Achilles Heel of asynchronous online learning, let me provide one tidbit of information that makes this drawback easier to take. Although asynchronous learning activities may take longer to conduct, parallel activities can be run simultaneously in different online group meetings. For example, I can create one meeting in which students are involved in a teaching activity called "Lifeboat." At the same time and in another meeting, a case-study discussion can be well on its way. In yet another meeting, students can be sharing and editing each other's research reports. Limits, of course, exist for this strategy, but running simultaneous activities in this way works more smoothly when students need not be in one scheduled location at a specific time.

Methods also exist for handling the frustrations inherent in delayed response time. Because the response time tends to scatter the focus of an online activity, keeping the students focused is important. This can take the form of asking open-ended questions during each day of the activity to help remind the students that you are watching the direction of the activity. Sometimes asking controversial questions during such activities motivates the students who might otherwise have remained equally uninvolved, to take a position.

The following activity works quite well in an asynchronous mode. Please note how the days are scheduled so that the asynchronous nature of online is taken into consideration.

Sample Online Activity: Field Trips through the Web

This activity allows the instructor to provide students with a guided tour to a city, park, or business website as if the instructor were taking students on a field trip. Special planning and scheduling on the part of the instructor are, of course, needed.

The objectives of this activity will:

- Provide students the opportunity to learn about other places via Internet websites.
- Help students become familiar with the various tourist-type websites available on the Internet.
- Teach students how to gather information on the Internet.

Materials will include:

- A list of places to visit, including their Internet addresses
- A set of unique activities for each student to perform while exploring an Internet site
- An Internet service provider (ISP) for each person in the class

The procedures of the activity involve the following:

Day 1:   Prepare the Students for Their Field Trip

Step #1:   Upload a lecture introducing the site selected for the field trip. Identify the theme of the field trip (e.g., historical, informational, scientific) so students know the purpose of the activity.

Step #2:   Provide the students with a travel agenda and timetable for visiting the places in the itinerary. It is also useful to provide students with unique assignments that may overlap slightly so that when they report their progress on Day 3, some information will be similar (for verification purposes) while other information is unique to a particular student.

Step #3:   Be sure to give students clear deadlines in terms of what should be accomplished by what day.

Day 2 through Day 5: Students Report the Results of Their Field Trip

Step #1:   By Day 3, students should send the results of the first phase of their field trip to the class forum for all to discuss. These results should include a summary of their experiences.

Step #2:   As the instructor, challenge some of the information presented. Encourage the students to question each other's data and experiences by visiting the areas discovered by other students.

Step #3:   On Day 4, prepare students for the final phase of their field trip. This phase would be due on Day 6.

Conclude the lesson by having students provide a three-paragraph summary of their Internet field trip. Ask the students to describe the advantages and disadvantages of going on an Internet field trip rather than visiting it in person.

The Importance of Daily Pacing

Daily pacing is very much connected with participation on the parts of both the instructor and the students. Online communication and learning depend on the visibility of the student so that the instructor knows that the student is in attendance. The students also need to know the instructor is there and is a part of the class.

Instructors and students new to this online learning tend to misunderstand the importance of maintaining visibility. Many onsite instructors are accustomed to wandering about the classroom during group discussions while listening in on each group to see how it is doing. In an onsite classroom, students are quite aware of the instructor's presence and even pick up the enthusiasm level of their discussion as the instructor nears their group. With physical presence, an instructor might use body language to motivate or communicate an idea to the class. Thus, an instructor can influence and even direct the students' learning just by being visible in the classroom. Many instructors take this aspect of physical presence for granted until they begin teaching online.

If an online instructor does not compensate for this hidden dependence on physical presence, students are quick to let administrators know. It begins with questions to other online students in their class: "Where is the instructor?" Within days of this first observation, students are feeling abandoned, even though the instructor may have been reading the online class discussion on a daily basis. When it comes to pacing and instructional participation, the rule is simple: If you are not participating (i.e., providing input to the class) and talking in this asynchronous classroom, you are not there. Out of sight is out of mind. The rule holds true for online students. An instructor should do everything possible to ensure that instructional and student input reach the classroom daily.

Does this mean that online instructors and students should send notes to the classroom every day? Let me answer this question by providing advice I often give students who are new to asynchronous, online education.

Fear of failure often begins with the question: Can I really learn this stuff? Should I be returning to school? Many students start off feeling that they cannot rise to this new learning endeavor. However, once they get going in the class, students soon discover that learning was never an issue; they have been in the learning mode their whole lives and being in school does not change this. What becomes the real challenge is the managing of one's time more effectively in an online class so one can continue with a real life outside the classroom.

I hope you will allow me to share how I manage online time. I have a technique that helps manage my online time, and it may work for many of you.

The way I like to organize my online time involves logging on daily. Doing this actually allows me to manage my time better. How? Well, if I wait a few days to log on, my mail box collects so many notes that it can take hours for me in one sitting to read through them and respond.

I don't know about you, but I don't have three or four hours in a day to read through and respond to all my notes. However, I do have one to two hours each day for online interaction. Interestingly, I find that I can manage my online time best by logging on each day. When I log on daily, I will spend one to two hours responding to messages. Since my daily schedule can handle one to two hours of online time, I feel more in control of how I manage time.

Of course, this does not include those extra homework assignments or reports. That is always going to take more time. However, if I can log on daily, I tend not to feel I'm in a catch-up mode.

If it works, let me know.

Students respond very positively to this message because as they get used to the asynchronous, online learning environment they begin to accept the need to log on daily to save time. In a way, time management is the salt and pepper of facilitating an online learning activity.

When preparing for an online activity, an instructor must provide very clear directions at least two days before the activity is to start. To do this, the instructor can set up participation requirements via a schedule of what is expected on a daily basis. The instructor can tell the students, for example, that on Day 2 they are expected to send the results of an assigned task to the class forum. On Day 4 they are to respond to tasks A and B. Online instructors can also make themselves accountable to such a pacing, as well. For example, the instructor can create a task list/schedule for when to send what to the class. Assigning certain handouts to be sent on a certain day of the class helps remind the instructor to be a part of the class as a contributor. Planning to send a particular question or more information during Day 3 of the class discussion not only helps the class discussion evolve and move along but it also adds to the consistency to how a class is taught. This method is one of the most efficient ways to help keep the pacing of the class moving.

Study the following online sample activity to see how an instructor might manage the pacing of an online class. Pay close attention to how many days occur between one set of assignments and another.

Sample Online Activity: Information Search

This exercise could take the form of a library search or a search for websites relevant to the course content. Each student is given a set of questions related to a specific course topic. Students then explore the university's online library to answer the questions.

Objectives of this activity will:

- Provide students the opportunity to navigate through Internet websites.
- Help students become familiar with the various search engines available on the Internet.
- Teach students the limitations of Internet searches.

This activity requires the following resources:

- Instructions for the exercise
- A list of information, terms, or websites to find.
- A list of techniques and tools on how to navigate the Internet

The procedures of the activity involve the following:

Day 1: Provide Students with a Lecture That Introduces the Main Search Engines Available on the Internet

Step #1:   Upload a lecture that provides the student with the task of identifying other search engines and their functions. Students should also be provided with a list of search items that they must locate on the Web. Some of these items can be found on the websites that the instructor introduced in the lecture. Other information (though available on the introduced search engines) must be found on websites that the students discover. The directions to the students can take the form mentioned in Step #2.

Step #2:   Provide students with a list of 20 items on which they must locate information on the Web. For 10 of these items, students may use the search engines introduced in the lecture to locate the information. The other 10 must be found on search engines or websites that students have discovered on their own.

Step #3:   As students locate each of the items, be sure they identify where they found them. This requires that students list the Web address where the information was located. All sites must be verifiable. If the website is no longer available when students turn in this assignment, they will not receive credit for that assignment.

Step #4:   Provide students with the following question to discuss for the next three days: What are the advantages and disadvantages of using the Internet as a research tool rather than the standard library?

Day 2 and Day 3:   Monitor the Class Discussion and Answer Questions

Step #1:   The instructor should pose the following discussion questions to the class at the end of Day 3: What has been the most challenging aspect of this exercise and how have you solved this challenge? What are some of the techniques and tools that you discovered so far?

Day 4 through Day 6:   Monitor the Class Discussion and Answer Questions

Step #1:   By the end of Day 6, the instructor should provide some of his or her own tips and tools that would help the students navigate the Internet.

Conclude the lesson by asking students to hand in the exercise list. Also instruct the students to send a brief summary to the main public forum for all to read and respond.

The Role of the Instructor

The role an instructor takes during any online learning activity will depend on the objectives of that activity. Some activities may be conducive to allowing the instructor to join as an equal participant, whereas others may not. The benefits will be discussed first.

Being the instructor who participates in an activity is yet another way to keep students on track and involved. Instructional participation allows the instructor to model the behavior that he or she would like the students to follow. I often set myself up as the point of attack during an online activity. For example, to force students to take and defend a position, I might take a stand that is obviously controversial. Although this technique may not be exclusive to online activities, since it is a common classroom teaching method, it is equally successful in an online class. Online students pull together the group energies and focus in on the instructor when the instructor participates as an equal contributor. Taking this position in an online learning activity also affords the instructor the opportunity to redirect the ideas without dominating the discussion. There have been many times when students have taken up discussing nonrelated topics. This results in perhaps 50 or so messages of reading on unrelated topics. Given that the average online class might generate 200 messages each day, having to read 50 irrelevant messages can become a source of frustration for both instructor and students, thus wasting everyone's time. To manage this, I, as a participant, bring up a controversial item and get the students on the attack in defending their positions. Another technique would be to force the content of the discussion by asking a leading question.

The potential downside of an instructor's participation brings up the possibility of the instructor dominating the group discussion. Since online learning is best as a facilitated experience rather than a place for an instructor's diatribe, the online instructor often wants to avoid becoming center to any group activity. Another drawback to an instructor's participation is that it often attracts those students who try to tell an instructor what they think the instructor wants to hear (i.e., "sucking up"). When either of these phenomena enters the class scene, the learning environment tends to get polluted and an instructor often finds himself or herself not knowing what the students are really thinking or learning from the experience.

This means that the instructor's decision whether to participate in a group activity will depend on the following:

- *The type of activity being run.*   If the exercise requires no specialized knowledge, then having the instructor participate as an equal player would not conflict with the facilitating pedagogy. If, however, the instructor is the expert, then he or she may want to take the role as guide rather than participant.
- *The student's age.*   If the students are traditional students, then the instructor might choose to guide more than participate. If, however, the students tend to be the nontraditional types, such as adults returning to school, then the instructor as an equal participant in an activity would be less likely to dominate the outcome.

The following activity is perfect for instructional participation. When I first used this exercise in an online setting, I sat outside the activity like a coach and directed the students on how they might respond. Directing the activity in this way often felt artificial and made the students feel like I was a kibitzer intruding in their world. Now that I participate in this activity like any of the other students, the whole dynamic of the discussion is better for the students. As a participant, I can control the flow, tone, and direction of the activity. Although I often get thrown out of the starship by the end of the exercise, students tell me that they get more out of it than those students who did the exercise without me.

Sample Online Activity: Space Colonists Exercise in Debating and Decision Making

The following exercise is organized for an asynchronous online classroom that runs for seven days. It is strongly recommended that the instructor participate as one of the players in this exercise, using it as an opportunity to provide direction or blatant examples of logical fallacies. Also, if the exercise is performed with a large class, small groups of eight can be created. Students can then be split into smaller class meetings where they can conduct the debate. When the exercise has concluded on Day 6, each group can select a leader to present the results and the rationale for each group's decision.

The exercise is derived from a well-known game called "Life Boat" or "Bomb Shelter." However, in this exercise, students play assigned characters. Furthermore, these characters are colonists on a starship on its way to a New World. Originally, the starship was designed to sustain 9 to 11 colonists for five years, which was the duration of the trip to the New World. Unfortunately, a meteor has struck the starship and damaged it, so there is now only enough oxygen for 5 colonists for the five-year period. As a result, the colonists must decide which 5 should stay and which should go.

The objectives of this activity will:

- Provide students the opportunity to argue logically.
- Help students learn to identify the logical fallacies in logical arguments.
- Teach students how generalizations and stereotypes can influence reasoning.
- Demonstrate how cultural norms influence perceptions.

This activity requires the following resources:

- Instructions for the exercise
- Character backgrounds for the students

The procedures of the activity involve:

Day 1: Send a Lecture on Logical Fallacies to the Online Class

The lecture touches on the following issues:

Step #1: How does one determine whether an argument is a good one? For example, in analyzing a reading, how does one know whether an author has made a strong argument? What does one look for? Fallacious reasoning can be one deficiency. Faulty induction or deduction can ruin the impact of an argument. Interestingly, some fallacies have happened so often that they have been identified and labeled. The most common fallacies are the following:

- *Hasty generalization.* This is a generalization accepted on the support of a sample that is too small or biased to warrant it. *Example:* All welfare recipients are lazy.
- *Post hoc ergo procter hoc.* This fallacy is a form of hasty generalization in which it is inferred that because one event followed another, it is necessarily caused by that event. *Example:* The rooster crowed, then the sun rose. Therefore the rooster caused the sun to rise.
- *Non sequitur.* In this fallacy, the premise has no direct relationship to the conclusion. This fallacy often appears in political speeches and advertising. *Example:* A waterfall in the background and a beautiful woman in the foreground have nothing to do with an automobile's performance.

- *Begging the question.* This is almost like an argument in a circle because the conclusion is assumed true for the premise to be accepted. *Example:* Of course, it is the word of God because God says so.
- *Contrary of fact hypothesis.* This fallacy is committed when a person states that if one event had not happened (when in fact it did), then things would be different. *Example:* If you didn't marry that idiot, you would be much better off today.
- *Ignoring the question.* This happens when the argument shifts from the original subject to a different one, or when the argument appeals to an emotional attitude that has nothing to do with the logic of the case. *Example:* No good American would approve of this communistic proposal.
- *False analogy.* This is an unsound form of an inductive argument where the argument is based completely on analogy to prove its point. *Example:* This must be a great car because, like the finest watches in the world, it was made in Switzerland.
- *Either/Or fallacy.* This fallacy assumes that one must choose between two opposite extremes instead of allowing for alternatives. *Example:* You are either for us or against us.
- *Common belief.* This fallacy is committed when one accepts a statement to be true on the evidence that many other people allegedly believe it. *Example:* Of course Lincoln was a great man. Everyone knows that.
- *Past belief.* This fallacy is similar to common belief except that the claim for the belief is support for it in the past. *Example:* Even the ancient Egyptians prepared for an afterlife. Therefore, there must be life after death.
- *Attacking the person.* This refers to attacking the arguer rather than his or her position. *Example:* John's objections to capital punishment carry no weight since he is a convicted felon himself.
- *Appeal to authority.* This tries to convince the listener by appealing to an expert who is often an authority in one field but who is speaking on a topic that is not within his area. *Example:* Bill Clinton says you should educate your children in public schools and he should know.
- *Bandwagon.* This fallacy appeals to the emotions and biases of the masses. It asks the listener to join the crowd of believers. *Example:* All our friends smoke. Should we smoke, too?
- *Red herring.* This fallacy introduces an irrelevant issue into the discussion as a diversionary tactic. *Example:* Many of the people say

that engineers need more practice in writing, but I would like to remind them how difficult it is to master all the math and drawing skills that an engineer requires.

- *Questionable cause.* This is committed when, without sufficient evidence, one identifies a cause for an occurrence. *Example:* That car in front of us is swerving side to side. The guy inside must be drunk.

- *Straw man.* This fallacy occurs when one misrepresents the opponent's position to make it easier to attack, usually by distorting the opponent's views to ridiculous extremes. (This is also called the *slippery slope* fallacy.) *Example:* Those who favor gun control legislation want to take all guns away from responsible citizens and put them in the hands of criminals.

- *Appeal to ignorance.* This is an argument to the effect that if something cannot be proven, then it must be false. *Example:* You cannot prove that there are no UFOs, so there must be some.

- *Two wrongs make a right.* This is committed when one tries to justify an apparently wrong action by charges of another wrong action. *Example:* The system stole money from me, so I should steal money from the system.

- *Amphibole.* This is a fallacy of language ambiguity that deliberately misuses implications. *Example:* Three out of four doctors recommend this type of pain relief. (The implied assertion here is that three out of four means 75 percent of all doctors and that this *type* of pain relief means this *particular* pain reliever.)

- *Equivocation.* This fallacy is a product of ambiguity. The arguer uses the ambiguous nature of a word or phrase to shift the meaning in such a way as to make the reason appear more convincing. *Example:* Sugar is an essential component of the body, a key material in all sorts of metabolic processes, so buy some XYZ sugar today.

- *Appeal to emotion.* In this fallacy, the arguer uses emotional appeal rather than logical reason to persuade the listener. The fallacy can appeal to various emotions, including pride, pity, fear, hate, vanity, or sympathy. *Example:* For just a dime a day, you can feed a starving child in Africa.

Step #2: Explain the following to the students:

You are colonists on a starship on its way to populate the New World. You are the sole survivors of the human race. You had to escape Earth because of a major catastrophe that destroyed your home planet.

Originally, the starship was designed to sustain 9 to 11 colonists for 5 years, which is the duration of the trip to the New World. Unfortunately, a meteor has struck the starship and damaged it, so that you now have only enough oxygen for 5 colonists for the 5-year period. As a result, you, the colonists, must decide which 5 should stay and which should go. You will each be assigned a character to play on Day 1. Each character will have a special background.

It is important that you first introduce your assigned characters to the group before Day 2. You must provide full disclosure of your character's background. You may embellish somewhat, but you cannot change the nature of the character's story. After all the students have introduced themselves as the characters they were assigned, the group must decide who should stay and who is to go. The discussion for this decision should begin by Day 3. Remember: The goal is to repopulate the New World, so you should keep this in mind when you are deciding. It is important to note that suicide is not permitted. You cannot volunteer to leave the spacecraft.

Step #3:   The instructor uploads the character assignments on Day 1. Allow the students one to two days to prepare reasons why they should stay in the starship. Instruct the students to take notes of logical fallacies as they listen to each other's arguments and counterarguments. Explain to the students that a class discussion on the fallacies that surface during the exercise will follow on Days 6 and 7.

Following is a list of characters for this exercise. Consider copying a description of each on a 3-inch by 5-inch index card. When you are ready to assign characters, have the student choose cards randomly.

Tell the students:

This is your character and story. When you introduce this character, do so in several paragraphs designed to present the information in a persuasive form. The information is skeletal, so you may embellish as long as you do not change the character's background.

> *Profession:*   Doctor
> *Age:*   63
> *Gender:*   Female
> *Story:*   You have an unusual memory problem. Although you can remember things when your memory works properly, there are days when you don't know who or where you are.

> *Profession:*   Radiation Expert
> *Age:*   44
> *Gender:*   Male
> *Story:*   You have had a violent temper and have killed people in the past. Doctors say you are fine now, but they won't guarantee anything.

Profession: Prostitute
Age: 28
Gender: Male
Story: You have multiple personalities. Doctors say you have as many as 20. Of these personalities, one claims to be a ghost. Further-more, the ghost personality tends to be the one that comes around the most.

Profession: Lawyer
Age: 27
Gender: Female
Story: You have terminal cancer and can die at any time within the next 10 years.

Profession: Nurse
Age: 30
Gender: Male
Story: You are 8½ feet tall and weigh over 400 pounds. You usu-ally eat twice as much as the normal person.

Profession: Air Force Pilot
Age: 38
Gender: Female
Story: Every now and then, you tend to sleepwalk all night. Some-times when you wake up, you are miles from where you went to sleep. Also, given that you have had extensive training as an escape artist when you were younger, you sometimes use these skills when you are asleep. Consequently, you have awakened inside sealed bank vaults, unaware of how you got in.

Profession: Police Officer
Age: 27
Gender: Male
Story: Your spouse recently died of the AIDS virus. You might be infected, but doctors had found no evidence because it was too early to say.

Profession: President of the United States of America
Age: 49
Gender: Female
Story: You dislike men so much that you can't stand being in the same room with them. Sometimes you even get a rash just being around them.

Profession: Psychiatrist
Age: 38
Gender: Male
Story: You have this annoying tendency to psychoanalyze every-one you speak with to the point that you have never had a social life. This would not be so bad except that because you don't know how to talk to people and never had any friends, you tended to write yourself prescrip-tions of drugs for recreational value. In fact, you did this so often that the drugs fried your immune system to such a degree that you get sick very easily. Sometimes the sickness can lead to a life-threatening illness such as pneumonia. If it were not for modern science, you probably would have died years ago.

Profession: Soldier
Age: 29
Gender: Male
Story: You were drunk and flying with an Air Force pilot over some part of the former Yugoslavia. Being too intoxicated to think straight, you pressed a button on the plane that dropped four nuclear devices on the countries below you. It is because of this accident that the super powers began shooting at each other. The result, of course, is a nuclear war that placed you all in this starship.

Profession: University Student
Age: 19
Gender: Female
Story: You are four months pregnant. Also before the war, a psy-chic told you that your child is the new savior.

Profession: Survival Expert
Age: 29
Gender: Male
Story: When you were younger, you were very concerned about the world's overpopulation problem. In order to do your part and not add to this growing population, you had an operation that now prevents you from fathering children.

Profession: Hairdresser
Age: 38
Gender: Female
Story: You were abducted by extraterrestrials that took you to their planet where they altered your genetic code. Upon your return to Earth, these aliens told you that you are now a superior human being. They also

told you that they would return two years after this holocaust to save you, explaining that they implanted a homing device in your body. Thus, as long as you are alive, this device is working and they will be able to find and save you and whoever is with you.

Day 2 through Day 5:   Give Students Five Days to Complete This Exercise.

Explain that there is a time limit and that a decision must be made before the end of Day 5.

Step #1:   Ask students to prepare a list of the fallacies. Perhaps a little competition could be started to see who identifies the most fallacies.

Step #2:   Be sure to provide as much input to the discussion as you would like the students to provide.

Step #3:   As the instructor, send a discussion comment at the end of Day 5. This comment should be a reminder that once the social aspect of the decision has been explored, the class should have a discussion on the types of fallacies that surfaced during this exercise.

Day 6 and Day 7:   Tabulate and Compare Results.

Invite discussion as to what social or cultural factors were at play in influencing decisions. For example, were some professions considered bad because of cultural norms? Open the discussion to the question of how participants from different cultures might come up with very different results.

Step #1:   Ask students to explain why certain fallacies may have been more convenient to use than others. If the issue has not already been discussed, explore how some of these fallacies might be tied to cultural perceptions and norms.

Step #2:   Ask students to list the fallacies they collected.
Conclude the lesson by emphasizing the source of fallacies and giving further examples of how perceptions can influence the way people evaluate information. Be sure to invite questions before ending the activity.

Conclusion

Learning activities can be used successfully in an online environment whether that environment is on the Internet or via an online conferencing system. For students who are new to online learning, the use of such activities is particularly beneficial. Nonetheless, the strength and potential weakness of this environment is in its asynchronous nature. Asynchronous learning involves working with and designing activities with the time delays in the communication flow in mind. This difference often catches many instructors transitioning to the asynchronous online class by surprise, especially when it comes to time management.

This chapter provided the instructor with some examples of successful online activities. An online educator must understand and use the asynchronous nature of online communication. Providing students with a daily schedule of events helps with the pacing so as to drive the students through each step of that activity. This daily pacing is very much connected with participation on the parts of both the instructor and the students. Online communication and learning depend on this sort of visibility. Finally, the instructor must decide if learning would be more effective if the instructor is an equal participant in or an observer of the activity. If an online instructor takes into consideration all the issues and samples presented in this chapter, then he or she is on his or her way to designing and conducting a successful online activity.

References

Kahane, H. (1992). *Logic and Contemporary Rhetoric: The Use of Reason in Everyday Life*. Belmont, CA: Wadsworth.

Reid, J. M. (1988). *The Process of Composition*. New York: Prentice-Hall.

Seech, Z. (1993). *Open Minds and Everyday Reasoning*. Belmont, CA: Wadsworth.

12

DEALING WITH CHALLENGING SITUATIONS
Communicating through Online Conflict

KEN WHITE

Some level of frustration and controversy is normal fare for faculty and students in the online learning environment. Online faculty often encounter difficult students who may dominate a class discussion, challenge course content, resent the authority or expertise of the instructor, display rude and inappropriate tone to other class members, refuse to adhere to the class structure and assignment schedule, or simply not participate. In addition, if conflicts are bad enough and are ignored long enough, the results can end up in the hands of administrators or even in a nasty lawsuit. The real task at hand is responding effectively to online conflicts before they get to the point where deans or attorneys are called in.

Although disagreement and conflict are inevitable aspects of all human relationships, the need to respond effectively in online conflict situations is particularly important. Sproull and Kiesler (1991) show that people interacting on computers are isolated from social cues and feel safe from surveillance and criticism. As a consequence of the low level of nonverbal and social information available online, messages are often startlingly blunt and discussions can easily escalate into name-calling and other forms of abusive and contemptuous behavior. Such "flaming" messages do not go unremarked, and can be met with numerous reactions that even resort to stronger language. Before the online instructor is even aware of a "flame war," the social fabric and learning climate of the class can be severely damaged.

Consequently, it is understandable if new online faculty members accept the long-held view that conflict is inherently negative and try to stay away from it. The fact that some online "talk" becomes more extreme and impulsive can be seen as revealing a weakness in the medium, a flaw in its design, operation, and communication processes. In an environment where students feel less bound by convention and less concerned with consequences, conflict can be seen as something to be avoided. Sources of conflict have to be identified and eliminated as soon as possible. Peace and stability have to be returned to the online classroom

The view of online conflict in this chapter is quite different. I want to emphasize that online conflicts are neither inherently negative nor positive; rather, it is what one makes of them. The focus of this chapter is on helping online teachers respond effectively to online conflict.

As a preface, I make a distinction between *reacting* and *responding*. I associate reactive behavior with the concept of *movement*. It is like a physical process found in nature. Like movement, reacting is reflexive—it is fight or flight. On the other hand, I consider responsive behavior more like the concept of *action*. It is a human practice involving thinking and choice. That is, responding is reflective. Unlike reptiles who react, humans are "response-able," able to respond.

Online conflict is responded effectively to (or not) through communication. As I will discuss later in this chapter, if one "reacts" to conflict, one ignores or cancels out a crucial communication element of conflict. By recognizing those communication elements, one can eliminate *reactive* or ineffective ways of communicating through online conflict and begin to *respond* effectively. One can benefit from reflecting on one's own attitudes about conflict and on one's communication skills, because while all online conflict is not rooted in poor communication, it always involves communication.

The starting point for responding effectively to online conflict is to ask yourself what it is you want to have happen. Focus on what is positive, specific, and practical. To begin, online conflicts can be responded to effectively by looking at three key areas: (1) What is online conflict and how does it work, including its benefits? (2) What are the different types of online conflict? and (3) What can online faculty and students do about each type?

Online Conflict as Communication

A few years ago, the American Management Association sponsored a survey of managerial interests in the area of conflict. The respondents in the survey were 116 chief executives, 76 vice presidents, and 66 middle managers. These executives and managers revealed what they considered to be the principal causes of conflict. Among the described causes were:

- Communication failure
- Personality clashes
- Value and goal differences
- Substandard performances
- Responsibility issues

Two important lessons for online teaching and learning can be drawn from the study. First, there are many grounds for conflict, and they are not limited to onsite situations. Whenever people are involved in interdependent and interactive relationships, such as the virtual or online organization, there are many situations over which conflicts can arise. Second, it may be quite challenging to get a handle on the complex and often subjective dynamics of conflict, particularly in the electronic classroom.

Consequently, the initial step in responding effectively to conflict situations is to know what the conflict is about and how it works. Once you have made some sense out of conflict and its communication dynamics, you are better able to figure out what you can do about it. I want to offer a communication-oriented definition of *conflict* that suggests specific ways for communicating through online conflict situations.

I agree with John Stewart of the University of Washington when he defines *conflict* as communication—verbally and nonverbally expressed disagreement between individuals or groups. Though broad, Stewart and D'Angelo's (1988) definition says several particular things about conflict. First, the definition points out that conflict is expressed with words or through nonverbal behaviors such as communication tone, which is an important factor in online communication. Sometimes, online students use words to express their disagreement by writing, "I disagree with what you are saying!" At other times, it is the lack of words and participation that clearly signal disagreement.

Second, when seen as communication, conflict is *expressed,* as opposed to being feelings that happen inside a person. The definition concentrates on communication, not on psychology. It does not encourage one to speculate about or interpret the motives of the person on the other end of the computer, but to focus on how both people communicate. It is a reminder that conflict is always about a relationship between two or more people.

Third, and most importantly, Stewart and D'Angelo's definition emphasizes that conflict is a natural part of human interaction. Conflict is essentially about different points of views. People have disagreements because they are different. Because they are not the same, and because they see and value things differently, people vary in their beliefs as to what things are or should be. Although conflict may divert time and energy away from tasks, represent the various issues that polarize individuals and groups within organizations, and obstruct cooperative action and decreases productivity, it is also a creative and positive force. It is important to recognize that, as communication, online conflict has some benefits.

Benefits of Online Conflict

If online conflict is inevitable and natural—if it represents the uniqueness of all people—then it is not always negative. If a major part of the problem about responding effectively with online conflict is one's tendency to think only about the negative part of it, then one needs to first do what I suggested in Chapter 1: "mutate your metaphors" about conflict. People need to begin seeing the benefits of online conflict.

The list of positive and creative values inherent in online conflict is equally long. Conflict has the potential to do the following:

- Open up hidden issues
- Clarify subject matter
- Improve the quality of problem solving
- Increase involvement in learning
- Increase cooperation and interaction

Online conflicts can be valuable and productive both for faculty and students. For the online instructor, conflict can stimulate creative problem solving, generate more effective ideas, and fine-tune learning relationships. For online students, conflict can provide opportunities to test, expand, and demonstrate skills; to better understand their co-learners; and to develop confidence and trust. Specifically, conflicts can help to do the following:

1. *Develop more interpersonal online relationships.*   There is a potential for human understanding that a legitimate disagreement can bring to the online classroom. Conflict can help people learn something new about each other and remind people of each other's humanity. One can develop understanding that goes beyond the subject matter of what one is learning to an appreciation of who one is. For example, say that there is a hidden conflict in an online ethics class about some students imposing their religious beliefs on others. In a discussion about the range of ethical theories, Richard declares that Christianity is the only true ethical viewpoint. He shares his Christian beliefs in every note he sends to the class discussion. He shows no sensitivity to other perspectives. Another student, John, is "silent" in the class, but eventually sends the instructor a personal message and writes in no uncertain terms, "If you don't stop this guy, I'm going to give him hell!"

The online instructor could avoid the possible benefit of conflict in this situation by ordering the class as a whole to respect all opinions and not to share their personal moral views. Instead, the instructor sends Richard a personal message and poses the problem to him. He describes the feelings and frustrations of the other students as well as one student's reluctance to join in the discussion, and asks how the situation should be handled. In response, Richard writes back that he does have strong beliefs, that he was not aware of the feelings of the other students, and that he will try to be less pushy. The instructor then supplements his communication with a telephone call to Richard, thanking him for his productive response and talking in more general terms about how the class is going, what the weather is like in Richard's hometown, and sharing personal information about jobs and family.

This example shows how online students often lack tangible reminders of their audience. Lacking the paralinguistic resources to help him convey his ideas, Richard resorted to even stronger language to express his passion of belief. Without a face to remind him of his audience and to temper his words, Richard forgot about convention and consequences. He needed to be reminded of the interpersonal element without increasing a sense of isolation that is common online. The instructor accomplished this by focusing on Richard's humanity, as well. Consequently, one result of the conflict was about tasks: a working relationship was formed. But a second result was even more important: Richard realized that he did not handle the interpersonal part of the online conflict very well—he did not remind himself of the person on the other end of the computer. The conflict taught him that he was "talking with" other people online who have feelings, thoughts, and lives of their own.

2. *Promote workable decisions in the online class.*   The adversary system of the country's courts operates on the assumption that truth and justice emerge from the clash of ideas. The preceding example shows how the

clash of ideas and disagreements can lead to more workable decisions in the online classroom. The instructor was able to get Richard to "own" the decision to temper his communication because the conflict was posed as a problem in need of a solution, not a conflict in need of resolution. If the instructor's decision to stop all sharing of personal moral viewpoints had been imposed, Richard and other students would have felt disenfranchised. They would have most certainly carried around increased feelings of isolation and resentments about the decision that could have interfered with future performance, cooperation, and decisions in the electronic classroom. The ultimate decision got the task completed and it strengthened relationships. In addition, Richard felt a part of the decision and was more likely to respect it. He realized that he was part of a real—though virtual—community.

3. *Help students realize that feelings exist online.*   Here I must emphasize that I am not talking about allowing online students to flame each other. It is crucial that feelings are communicated productively online. I am talking about opportunities to express and explain feelings through respectful language. Online conflicts, if responded to effectively, can be positive opportunities for getting feelings out in a medium that is mostly assumed to be impersonal. Dealing with feelings shows students the human element that is always present in the online environment. As the previous example shows, if the energy of a feeling such as anger can be channeled into a positive communication framework, the feelings can be used to find creative solutions and more complete human relationships.

4. *Promote confidence in online learning.*   There is always uncertainty in a person when things really get difficult. The first serious argument with another student or instructor is a major event. This is especially true in online learning situations where the phenomenon of flaming suggests that communication becomes more extreme and impulsive. But the confidence that follows a well-managed online conflict can be extremely valuable to learning. It is often those educational encounters that avoid conflict that are ultimately the most insecure and unproductive because they remain untested. Both online students in the preceding example felt a new sureness, a new security, in their working relationship. Their online relationship was tested by conflict, and they had the opportunity to develop trust and confidence by learning how to communicate successfully through those conflicts. They ultimately recognized the value of the experience and the important learning that took place.

Of course, a positive attitude is the first step to responding effectively to online conflict. Faculty and students need to begin seeing conflict as creative and productive. The second step is to recognize that online conflict comes in several types.

Types of Online Conflict

Conflict is a pervasive part of all human relationships, including those in the electronic classroom. In fact, some philosophers have suggested that it is what makes humans human. All people are different, and conflict is just a reflection of that natural condition. To eliminate conflict online would mean eliminating its most human element. Without differences, online learning would not be an interpersonal activity.

But in order to respond effectively through online conflict, faculty and students also need to recognize that not all disagreement is the same. There are three basic types of online conflict:

1. *There is conflict over facts or interpretations.*   This kind of disagreement reflects differing views over the content and expectations of an online course; it is disagreements over fact. People can disagree over the fact that Columbus landed in the Western Hemisphere in 1492 (which can easily be confirmed or disconfirmed) or they can disagree over meaning—whether he "discovered" America at all (which is a matter of interpretation). The most important question to ask yourself when dealing with this type of online conflict is: What level of conflict are you disagreeing about—fact or meaning? It makes a difference. Your syllabus may say that students are required to interact in the online class, but what does *interaction* mean? Is a student who always responds to other student comments with short statements such as "I agree" actually interacting? And what is "correct grammar" online? Should online discussion be evaluated by the same grammatical standards as more formal online assignments such as term papers or case studies? Or are online discussions, although textual, more like conversations? In addition, what does "page" mean online? Is a page one screen or is it a traditional page in length? These kinds of small conflicts over facts and interpretations can be very disruptive in an online class until they are discussed and clarified. In fact, flaming is often a consequence of different interpretations of words.

One fundamental online conflict over facts or interpretation can be about what, exactly, an *online class* is. Generally speaking, an online course can be accessed anywhere and anytime and makes use of computer technology to deliver student learning at flexible times and places. But some online classes do not require any attendance or participation—resembling "correspondence courses" more than structured educational experiences that include interaction with faculty and other students, due dates, institutional support, and the kinds of materials that contribute to the development of a full course. Many online students enter programs with their own definitions of what an online course is; thus, there is an immediate need to clarify the nature of the course and the roles of faculty members and students.

2. *There is conflict over online roles and identities.* This kind of disagreement particularly reflects differing perspectives over the roles of online instructors. Cues in traditional educational settings reinforce social differences. An instructor lecturing at the front of a classroom or meeting a student in an office is a reminder of status differences. Online technologies weaken social differences apparent in face-to-face communication. Online instructors are not awarded authority or expertise by students simply because instructors look the part. All online messages have an equal status to a certain degree because they look alike. The only thing that can set them apart is their content, or what William James might call their "cash value." Without the "halo effect" of status, the competence and ability of the online instructor are in question from the beginning of class and are only earned through the quality of messages and how informative they are. While traditional students in a regular classroom might tend to accept the instructor's viewpoints as authority, online students more readily tend to question and challenge instructor opinions.

Consequently, many online conflicts about roles and identities focus on whether an instructor is considered informed or uninformed or are centered on who has what kind of authority with a given topic. Being labeled by students as informed is an important step in defining your position as the online instructor, but that is balanced against similar needs of many online students. Many online students are working adults in established careers. They have learned enormously from certain important work and other life experiences. They have learned a great deal in ways other than taking courses. They are the "experts" in many topics. This experience needs to be recognized and utilized by the online instructor. That is why many instructors prefer to identify themselves as *facilitators,* understanding that online conflicts around power relationships can be understood as struggles over such identities and roles. Stewart and D'Angelo say that (1988) communication is often about the "negotiation-of-selves."

3. *There is conflict over values.* Online instructors recognize that online classes are part of social organizations as well as places where people accomplish individual and collective tasks. Over a time period, most organizations develop a culture that strongly affects the way people view their places of work, its management, and its primary purposes. Although *cul-*

ture in organizations is defined as the common values of both managers and employees, cultural values are not imposed. They are developed over time. There can be disagreements over organizational values, such as over the level of expectations of all members of the staff, and regarding what *service to customers* means. In fact, conflict over cultural values may be necessary. Communication and human relations in organizations with well-defined, positive cultural values are nearly always better than in those that pay little attention to the values of the organization. There is value in communicating through conflict about organizational values. But they are most effectively dealt with in a structured way where there is an opportunity for mutual respect, learning, and maintaining interpersonal relationships.

As suggested earlier, the values of various online programs differ. For example, is *education* a value? It is clear that many working adults who enter online programs do not really want the education—they want what the education provides for them in better jobs, moving up the career ladder, and the ability to communicate ideas. But are those the values of the particular online programs they enter? If a student enters your class with these values, and you expect an "intellectual life," then there might be a conflict over values.

Ultimately, the main point is to know your conflict. But whatever the type of conflict, the next step in responding effectively is knowing what to do, or knowing what *not* to do—reacting.

Reacting to Online Conflict

Going back to the beginning of this chapter and the distinction made between *reacting* and *responding,* the following ways of dealing with online conflict can be identified as "reactive." A reactive approach does not see that whenever there is disagreement, there are always four elements to the conflict: (1) you, (2) the other person, (3) the topic, and (4) the climate. Figure 12.1 illustrates a circle where each one of the conflict elements makes up one quarter of the circle. In order for the circle to be whole, it must include every element.

The first three elements of conflict are easy to understand. The *you* of a conflict is anyone who deals with the second part of conflict—*other people.* The *topic,* of course, is the subject of what you and others are talking about. The *climate* of a conflict can be the physical environment and objects (on the phone, face to face, in the kitchen or office, on the computer, the temperature of the room) but also the emotional level of the topic.

FIGURE 12.1   The Four Elements of Online Conflict

Satir (1972) defines the reactive styles in four ways:

1. *"Placating" is when you ignore yourself in online conflict.*   Placating is an example of denying that a conflict exists. It is unresponsive because it fails to acknowledge disagreement. It avoids the conflict by using statements that terminate "talk" about the conflict before the discussion has thoroughly developed. It writes in generalities and avoids specific. When online instructors or students placate a conflict, they do not directly accept their responsibility. Often, online placators lurk in the background of the class, simply observing and keeping their opinions to themselves.

2. *"Pouncing" is when you try to ignore or eliminate the other person in the online conflict.*   Pouncing or blaming another person is a way of driving him or her away from the disagreement. It is when you want the other person to placate. Flaming, the online equal of pouncing, is often based on the belief that your view is the only "right" one. Some signs of flaming include name-calling, rejection, hostile questioning, hostile joking, and accusations. Flaming is an example of controlling an online conflict. It is unresponsive because it fails to acknowledge the other person's opinions. When people flame, they tend to communicate with an air of superiority and intimidation. They can run the gamut from "deadly quiet" to sarcastic and "loud." Often, they type in ALL CAPS, which is interpreted as yelling online. Pouncers—online flamers—are so intent on being right that they do not really read what other online students are writing, even when asked a direct question.

3. *"Distracting" is when you try to change the subject of the online conflict.* Distracting assumes that if you change the subject, the conflict will go away. It doesn't. The clearest sign of distracting is an abrupt change of the topic. One example is when the online student substitutes social chat for substantive responses to discussion questions. This conflict usually centers on the person's role as an online student. Many people enter online learning programs expecting a "correspondence course" experience. Often, what they find is a structured educational experience with required social interaction and expectations for contributing to the understanding of a subject matter. If an online student is not prepared for such a role (which is the conflict), he or she often responds with social chat or low participation. The online instructor must recognize the distracting nature of this behavior and encourage the student to contribute by asking specific questions that will move the student forward or by addressing the issue through personal messages. But the conflict must be recognized. Online instructors need to be prepared for angry responses when such a student is pushed to contribute more significantly or when the issue is raised through a personal message. Such distracting is an example of diverting a underlying conflict.

4. *"Computing" is when you try to ignore the emotional climate of the online conflict.* Computing is an example of not only ignoring the human potential of online learning, but further dehumanizing an online conflict. It is unresponsive because it fails to acknowledge the feelings of a real person on the other end of the computer. It sees the online environment as simply technical, not interpersonal. When people compute, they tend to remain impersonal. They use jargon and technical language. Often, they want to deal only with "the cold, hard facts." They are so intent on being detached that they often talk in the third person and show little awareness of audience and personal voice. Instead of seeing what others in the class are up to, and writing more as dialogue, they remain abstract.

Conclusion: Responding Effectively to Online Conflict

The most effective way to communicate through conflict is by *responding*. It is communication that "responds" to all four parts of the conflict: you, the other, the topic, and the climate. It responds to feelings and "stands up for its own rights," it responds to the student by asking about and listening for feelings and attitudes, and it "sticks to the topic." Finally, it responds to the emotional climate of the conflict by recognizing that feelings have a place online.

I conclude this chapter with some suggestions offered by Sillars and colleagues (1982) that can be directly applied to the online class. Responding effectively to online conflict can be practiced by using certain kinds of interpersonal and supportive statements. These include:

- *Using descriptive language.* Statements about observable events and behaviors related to the conflict should be nonevaluative. For example, you might write a note such as the following to a student's personal mailbox: "I feel that you were trying to be humorous with this statement, but it can come across as sarcastic to some people. What do you think?" Or if you are dealing with late assignments: "My records indicate that I did not receive your weekly summary assignment. Is that correct?" Descriptive language tends to be tentative.
- *Setting limits.* Statements should explicitly qualify the nature and extent of the conflict as well as set clear boundaries. If an online student has been disruptive, you might first make a comment in the main meeting room, letting all students know the expectations of higher education and of the class. This step allows the student to save face while being informed of important limits. If this does not work, then you can telephone the student or send a message via his or her personal mailbox. The syllabus is the most important place to lay out clear boundaries for the class, particularly regarding tone, student responsibilities, quantity and quality of participation, cheating, grading, and late work.
- *Offering support.* Statements should express understanding, acceptance, or positive regard for the other person. I often send messages to the main meeting that tells students how much I appreciate the tone of their online communication. In this way, I attempt to establish some cultural norms for the class. I also address process issues as well as content in my feedback.
- *Emphasizing commonalties and relationship reminders.* Statements should comment on common ground. I often send a message to the main meeting where I will say something like the following: "As a member of this class, I'm feeling uncomfortable with the tone of the present conversation. I'm feeling that some people could interpret it as sarcastic. What does everyone else feel?" In this message, I emphasize our common ground as members of the class and as human beings with feelings. I remind online students that conflict exists within a broader context of mutual commitment, respect, understanding, and learning.
- *Initiating problem solving.* Statements should initiate mutual consideration of solutions. If there is a conflict between two students, I contact them both privately either through their private mailboxes or by telephone. I attempt to describe what I see and ask them how the problem can be solved.
- *Fractionating.* Break conflicts down from one big mass into several smaller pieces. Stay very specific. Do not interpret a poor use of words

as a value conflict. Attempt to address the conflict by contacting the student through his or her personal mailbox or telephone before it emerges in the main meeting.

- *Defusing.* Continually ask yourself: "How well am I responding to conflict?" Defusing is reading notes carefully, identifying areas of agreement, and maintaining a positive tone. By listening carefully and communicating your own values cautiously, you can help create a sense of trust and mutual respect for differences in the online classroom.

But remember, most of all, you can respond most effectively to online conflict by remembering conflict is an important learning opportunity.

References

Satir, V. (1972). *Peoplemaking*. Palo Alto, CA: Science and Behavior Books.

Sillers, A. L., Coletti, S. F., Parry, D., & Rogers, M. A. (1982, Fall). Coding verbal conflict tactics: Nonverbal and perceptual correlates of the "avoidance-distributive-integrative" distinction. *Human Communication Research, 9,* 83–95.

Sproull, L., & Kiesler, S. (1991). *Connections: New Ways of Working in the Networked Organization*. Cambridge, MA: The MIT Press.

Stewart, J., & D'Angelo, G. (1988). *Together: Communicating Interpersonally.* New York: Random House.

13

ONE DAY LEFT TO LIVE
Teaching the Online Quantitative Course

JIM FARRAR

If I had only one day left to live, I would want to spend it in my statistics class—it would make it seem so much longer.—Author unknown

As the above quote indicates, the bad news is that quantitative courses generally strike fear in the hearts of many students. And as online quantitative instructors know, the online classroom exacerbates that fear. The main challenge for the online quantitative instructor is to smooth the turbulent waters and to help students focus on the subject in a difficult learning environment. The good news is that there are ways the online instructor can do so.

Although there are numerous technical questions about the online quantitative course that could be considered in this chapter, I choose to limit it to one question: *How can the online quantitative instructor present mathematical information to students in a clear and interactive manner?* Implied in this question is the understanding that, like any teaching medium, the online classroom has its advantages and disadvantages, particularly for mathematical subject matter. For example, the online class is accessible to group work that not only can enhance the electronic medium for students but can teach them math, as well. On the other hand, while the online medium opens up countless opportunities for working adult learners, its textual and graphic capabilities constrain some forms of instructional communication. In particular, it often limits the ways the quantitative instructor can present mathematical concepts and information.

In this chapter, I will discuss issues related to teaching quantitative concepts effectively in the online environment such as preparing students for the online quantitative course, presenting an online lesson, and using small groups in the quantitative course to enhance student understanding.

Teaching Quantitative Concepts in the Online Course

Teaching online quantitative courses is a different matter from teaching in more traditional settings. I have taught for the University of Phoenix in both onsite and online classrooms. I started with the university in 1981, taught at the onsite Phoenix Campus until 1991, and was later invited to teach for the Online Campus. I have taught and developed statistics, finance, and technology management courses for both the onsite and online environment.

Although teaching onsite courses can be labor intensive and time consuming, online quantitative courses are intensified because they are not bound by the same standards of time and space. As an online instructor, I spend an average of two hours each day reading and responding to students' notes. This is in addition to my initial preparation time for the course syllabus, weekly lecture material to supplement the textbook, and other materials needed by the students. I also spend about two or three hours a week reviewing, grading, and preparing feedback to each student.

In both the onsite and online environment, the students seem to learn the formulas and concepts of the quantitative course best through anecdotal examples. In the onsite classroom, these are usually introduced in the first week of the class through a formal presentation, using slides and examples on the board. However, in the online classroom, concepts are often presented in note form, using American Standard Code for Information Interchange (ASCII) text files. ASCII files are standard for representing text in computers. Many computers can understand ASCII-coded files (plain text), whereas they might not understand files that were coded by programs such as word processors or spreadsheets (formatted), although these programs usually can have an option to save files in ASCII format. ASCII files are sometimes referred to as *text files* or *plain text files*.

Presentation is the main challenge for the online quantitative instructor, as students are not required to have and many do not have the same software as the instructor. The only common option becomes ASCII text files. In order to communicate effectively and consistently with every student in the class, online instructors are required to use the ASCII option.

Unfortunately, this eliminates the formatted file option that is capable of sending sophisticated mathematical symbols, forces the student to depend on the textbook for the formulas, and raises the anxiety level. But the limitation can be partially overcome with ASCII files by using a substitute mathematical language, for example, *x bar* for $X|$.

Here are some other examples:

Example 1

When using the following equation used to calculate the sample mean of a group of numbers,

$$\bar{X} = \frac{\sum X}{n}$$

where $\bar{X}$ is the sample mean, Σ represents summation, X represents the values in the sample, and *n* is the number of values in the sample. When limited to ASCII, one has to write the following text to describe the equation:

X bar = Sum (X)/n

Although the ASCII text does represent the equation, it obviously looks different from that in the students' text and adds some confusion. It would be ideal if the equation could be included in the online lecture as a formatted file in the same form as the textbook, and remove much of the frustration. But plain text does get the job done. Here's another example:

Example 2

When using the following equation to calculate the weighted mean for a set of numbers,

$$\bar{X_w} = \frac{\sum (w \cdot X)}{\sum w}$$

in ASCII text format, it would look something like this:

X subw bar = Sum(w times X)/Sum w

Again, it is much easier to view the formatted equation and compare it to what the text might have than it is to try and relate it to the ASCII version. Here is one more example:

Example 3

When using the following equation to calculate the standard deviation of a sample of values,

$$\sigma = \sqrt{\dfrac{\displaystyle\sum_{i=1}^{N} (X - \mu)^2}{N}}$$

the ASCII version looks like this:

omega = square root (sum [(x – mu) squared]/N)

I hope it is clear by now that the more complicated the formulas become, the more difficult it is to prepare an ASCII equivalent. Suffice it to say that the online class would be much easier on both student and faculty if it could be taught in an environment where formatted notes can be utilized. Again, while the University of Phoenix's conferencing software will support both the ASCII format and fully formatted attachments, many students do not have the appropriate software and often experience problems with attachments. In summary, though problematic, it is simply more convenient for the online quantitative instructor to use plain text files.

Preparing the Online Student for the Quantitative Course

As other contributors in this book have observed, it is essential for online instructors to set a personal tone to compensate for the constraints of the technology and communication. This is even more crucial in the high-anxiety atmosphere of the online quantitative course.

As an introduction to my online statistics course, I give students the following information to encourage them to focus on concepts and not be intimidated by the mathematical concepts or the stark electronic medium. I begin by observing that those students who have used statistics in the real world know that they do not use formulas and tables to do the work—they enter the data into a computer software package, select the appropriate statistical procedure, and interpret the output. But as such a user, I also know that it is important to understand how and when specific statistical tests should be used and how to interpret the results of these tests. Therefore, the objective of the class is not only for students to understand the concepts that underlie statistical tests but also to know when these tests should be used.

I then emphasize that in the online medium, when students are stumped on a particular concept, it takes time to get them help. Consequently, there is a real need for me to be online five out of seven days in order to keep on top of student progress and problems. I add that I am also open to calling or receiving phone calls from struggling students. I know, as any math instructor knows, that if one student is struggling with a concept, there is a good chance others are, as well. That is why I continually post extra examples of worked problems as often as I can.

In addition, I tell students that reading a quantitative textbook is much different from reading other texts. Quantitative material often takes several readings and ongoing practice before the material is fully understood. This is an important observation, because the typical working adult online student does his or her reading in the evening after they arrive home, have some dinner, and spend some time with their families. They are often tired after a full day at work, and when they discover they are not grasping the material on the first reading, they become frustrated and discouraged.

It is important, then, for me to stress that the quantitative subject may not be like most subjects students have studied. Some quantitative concepts are simple and straightforward; others are incomprehensible. There is usually no middle ground. This dichotomy can be very frustrating to the working adult student. In my own experience, I have often read over a single sentence several times, then suddenly, everything falls into place. I encourage online students to find a way to deal with the frustration until they can get over these hurdles. For example, I know that working adult students often try to study while other things are going on around them. I suggest to students that they choose a quiet place away from activity and add some soothing background music to mask any distracting noises. In addition, many people can do quantitative work only when they are at their peaks, and not for long periods of time. Studying in the evening may not be the most productive time. I suggest that it might be wise to try to block out one to two hours in the early morning and see if that helps.

There are several other techniques online quantitative students can adopt to make the work more beneficial and pleasurable. I recommend the following to all students, adding a little humor:

1. Scan the reading assignment to get the general idea of the content.
2. Read and reread the syllabus and lecture notes carefully to determine where to focus attention.
3. Reread the reading assignment.
4. Do the exercises early in the week and submit questions as soon as you can.

5. Use the information from other student questions and observations.
6. Before submitting the assignments, review them to ensure all work has been completed.
7. It's Miller time! (Optional)
8. Do not go to step 7 early! It does not work well.

Finally, I stress that my feedback will be provided on a timely and regular basis. Online students are scattered over the entire country and often around the world. They are essentially out there alone with computer messages as a lifeline. This requires that feedback be timely and substantive. Daily feedback is often required. Questions require direct answers citing specific examples in the text and, in many cases, examples of how the concept or formula is applied. I want my students to know that I will be there for them.

A Sample Online Lecture on Measures of Central Tendency

There are teaching techniques available to the online faculty member in the quantitative class. Foremost, I handle the issues that are associated with not being able to work problems in front of the students by providing good lecture notes and one or two examples of the major types of problems to be covered during each week. This requires substantial work up front, but once it is done for a given class, it does not usually have to be done again, unless there is a major revision to the course.

Following is a sample online lecture that demonstrates a relatively simple statistical concept and an example problem. As a whole, I do not re-create equations in their entirety in ASCII text. I just take the components and discuss how they work within the equation. Not only does this make the software limitations manageable but it also makes the student think about what is actually happening in the mathematical formula. The approach can easily be used in any online quantitative courses—finance, statistics, economics, and others. It is not intended to be all-inclusive, but to show a typical online quantitative lesson.

Measures of Central Tendency

Sets of data will show a tendency to group or cluster about a certain point. For a particular set of data, it is usually possible to select some typical value of average to describe the data set. This descriptive value is a measure of central tendency or location.

There are several averages used as measures of central tendency: The arithmetic mean, the median, and the mode are examples. The arithmetic mean (or simply the mean) is the most commonly used measure of central tendency. It is calculated by summing all the observations in a set of data and then dividing that sum by the total number of observations. The general equation for the arithmetic mean is 2.4 in your text on page 63. Here, X bar represents the mean (what we're calculating); sigma (the Greek letter) indicates a summation. The i = 1 and n notation (on the bottom and top of the sigma respectively) mean that we are going to add all n values in our observation (1 through n). X sub i represents each observation, in turn, and n is the number of observations. Let's apply a concrete example.

A sample of five executives received the following individual bonus amounts last year: $14,000, $16,000, $17,000, $19,000, and $21,000. Find the average (arithmetic mean) for these five amounts.

Our sample contains 5 observations, or pieces of data, therefore n = 5. Let's assign Xsub1 to be $14,000, Xsub2 = $16,000, and so on up to Xsub5 = $21,000. (I do this step only to emphasize the meaning of the notation Xsubi.) Now, as equation 2.4 indicates, we'll sum all values Xsub1 through Xsub5.

$$
\begin{array}{r}
14,000 \\
16,000 \\
17,000 \\
19,000 \\
+21,000 \\
\hline
87,000
\end{array}
$$

To complete the process, we divide by 5 (our value for n in this sample.) 87,000/5 = 17,400. Thus,

$$Xbar = \$17,400$$

Notice that it is unnecessary to carry units along in our calculation. In this instance, our units are dollars, and we can simply state this in our answer.

Now that we have calculated the arithmetic mean for the given sample problem, we can summarize some important facts about the mean.

1. Every set of interval-level and ratio-level data has a mean. (See section 1.3 in your text to refresh your memory! Are the amounts in this sample interval or ratio-level data?)

2. All data values are included in computing the mean.
3. Every set of data has a unique mean.
4. The mean is affected by unusually large or small data values.
5. The arithmetic mean is the only measure of central tendency where the sum of the deviations of each value from the mean is zero.

Let's prove to ourselves that statement 5 is true while at the same time doing a little work toward our next calculation, standard deviation given by equation 2.6 on page 58 of the text. First, find the difference between each bonus amount given in our example and the mean that we calculated from that data (Xsubi – Xbar).

$$14,000 - 17,400 = -3,400$$
$$16,000 - 17,400 = -1,400$$
$$17,000 - 17,400 = -400$$
$$19,000 - 17,400 = 1,600$$
$$21,000 - 17,400 = 3,600$$

If you add these amounts together, keeping in mind the negative numbers, you will indeed come up with zero. We have also just figured the individual deviations from the mean, the first step in finding the standard deviation. The notation in equation 2.6 is the same as in our equation for arithmetic mean—we've just done a couple of extra operations on our data. For instance, we are now finding individual deviation values and squaring each of them before performing the summation. Let's go through this equation step by step:

1. Calculate the difference between each observation in the data set and the mean value. (We just did that for our sample problem.)
2. Square each difference.
3. Add the squared results together.
4. Divide the summation by $(n - 1)$.

At this point, we have the variance, defined as the average of the sum of squared deviations around the mean. To get the standard deviation, move on to step 5.

5. Take the square root of the variance.

Not to beat a dead horse, but let's use our example one more time to compute standard deviation for our set of data. Having already calculated the difference between each observation and the mean value, we'll pick up where we left off, at step 2:

$$(-3,400)(-3,400) = 11,560,000$$
$$(-1,400)(-1,400) = 1,960,000$$
$$(-400)(-400) = 160,000$$
$$(1,600)(1,600) = 2,560,000$$
$$(3,600)(3,600) = 12,960,000$$
$$\text{Total} = 29,200,000$$

Divide the total by 4 (our value for $n - 1$):

$$29,200,000/4 = 7,300,000$$

On to our final step, take the square root of 7,300,000 and we have a standard deviation of:

$$S = \$2702.00 \text{ (rounded to the dollar)}$$

The standard deviation gives us an idea of the distribution of the data around the arithmetic mean. A large standard deviation tells us that our data had great variability, while a small S indicates little variability.

Using Study Groups in the Online Environment

As you can see, teaching an online quantitative course has the potential for being as dry as reading the information in a textbook. One way of enhancing the quantitative course is through the use of small group instruction. Students who participate in small groups experience a significantly greater increase in confidence in mathematical ability than students who participate only in the lecture method of instruction (DePree, 1998). As in onsite classes, online teaching strategies that promote a cooperative rather than a competitive learning environment enable students to make sense of mathematical thinking and enjoy the experience more.

There are many benefits to using small groups in quantitative courses. The University of Phoenix encourages the use of study groups as a way to foster a collaborative and cooperative spirit in the classroom and in the

Note: Material in this section was adapted from a summary of University of Phoenix Guidelines for Developing Online Course Modules; Goals of Online Module Development. Used with permission.

workplace. Group work helps reduce the sense of isolation experienced in both traditional and electronic settings. Students benefit from the social interaction of small group instruction. They can help each other in ways that the instructor cannot. Peers often see the trouble other students are having more clearly than the instructor does.

I generally use study group activities in my online quantitative classes to give the students the benefit of using the "two heads are better than one" approach. It is my experience that online students experience a greater sense of mathematical achievement when they participate in small groups. Working with others helps students understand mathematical concepts by comparing results and interacting with others.

In addition, I use online study groups to help alleviate time demands. Group work frees up time and allows me to direct students to each other as problem solvers. I am no longer the sole authority. Study groups encourage students to see each other as resources and give me the time to concentrate on those students most in need of help. As Donald Finkel and Stephen Monk (1983) observe, the most striking consequence of allowing students to interact directly in small groups with subject matter without my mediation is that I come face to face with the students' own partially formed and inadequate conceptions of the subject.

On the other hand, although group activities seem to be well suited to process-oriented courses such as human relations, management, organizational development, and ethics, they can be awkward in "number-crunching," task-oriented courses such as accounting, statistics, finance, and research. Group activities can become quite frustrating in the online quantitative course. Simply at the logistical level, it is more complicated than onsite groups. For example, I have to create meetings that "branch" off the main meeting place and invite only those students in that particular group. (Note that it is important that your software allows you to create your own meetings. Without this capability, there will be no opportunity for virtual groups.) Then students have to join those branch meetings. As an online instructor, this means that my list of meetings that I have to attend and monitor grows and data management becomes crucial.

In addition, consensus building and decision making are also more time consuming in asynchronous settings than in traditional classes. The logistics of online students simply agreeing on whom should complete specific tasks takes time. Moreover, time zone differences contribute to delayed interaction and reaction making the online group process cumbersome and sluggish.

Consequently, I limit the scope of group assignments and the number of students in each group to three or four, though the size of each group varies some according to the type of project and the expertise of the students. I also try to prepare students for online group work by doing the following:

- Explaining why group work is relevant in the quantitative course
- Helping students set up realistic expectations
- Observing or "lurking" in each group and offering advice
- Providing immediate feedback

I often assign short group projects that ask online students to dig a little deeper into a concept and techniques for analysis. This involves setting up a number of branch meetings and inviting three to four students to each branch. Students are given an assignment and are required to work together to solve the assignment's problem. The textual format of online learning allows me to follow the logical progression of each group and the thinking of individuals, as well as to interject ideas along the way. After each group has completed the assignment, the group is required to upload a template to the general class meeting where groups can compare results.

Most importantly, when I choose a group assignment, I limit the complexity and the scope of the project to ensure that it is manageable within the time frame of the class. Some group assignments and projects due in one week or less create a high level of anxiety among students. Consequently, I often combine what would normally be weekly group assignments in an onsite class into either one or two group assignments for the online class.

Finally, guidelines for the use of small groups in quantitative courses can be drawn from works such as Johnson and Johnson (1990) and Bruder (1990). There are numerous team-building exercises and math activities designed for use with small groups and transferable to the online environment. Again, your software should allow for the creation of separate, or branch, meetings. But if the technology permits, online instructors can easily create ways to better facilitate group work in quantitative courses.

Conclusion

The National Council of Teachers of Mathematics (1991) states that the shift from an industrial society to an information society has transformed the field of mathematics education. The critical components of mathematics curricula are now problem solving and conceptual understanding. The current emphasis is on active learning that encourages mathematical discourse.

The online classroom offers valuable learning experiences for working adult students in quantitative courses. The online medium plays an important part in a transformed mathematical education that promotes problem solving, conceptual understanding, and quantitative discourse. As a means for cooperative, small group methods, online education provides a supportive learning environment in which working adult students can learn what they need to know about mathematics and deepen their sense of possibilities.

References

Bruder, I. (1990). Putting math reform to work. *Electronic Learning, 10* (3), 18–19.

DePree, J. (1998). Small-group instruction: Impact on basic algebra students. *Journal of Developmental Education, 22* (1), 2–6.

Finkel, D. L., & Monk, G. S. (1983). Teachers and learning groups: Dissolution of the atlas complex. *New Directions for Teaching and Learning, 14,* 83–97.

Johnson, D. W., & Johnson, R. T. (1990). Using cooperative learning in math. In N. Davidson (Ed.), *Cooperative Learning in Mathematics: A Handbook for Teachers.* Menlo Park, CA: Addison Wesley.

National Council of Teachers of Mathematics. (1991). *Professional Standards for Teaching Mathematics.* Reston, VA: Author.

14

MAKING SENSE OF IT ALL

Giving and Getting Online Course Feedback

FRED SCHWARTZ AND KEN WHITE

In 1987, Arthur W. Chickering and Zelda Gamson published *Seven Principles for Good Practice,* distilled from decades of research on learning in higher education. Principle number four states, "Good practice in undergraduate education...gives prompt feedback" (Chickering & Gamson, 1987).

Prompt feedback recognizes that undergraduate students need to know what they know and do not know in order to focus their learning. Students need help in assessing existing knowledge and performance, as well as opportunities to get suggestions for improvement. They need to reflect on what they have learned, what they still need to learn, and how to evaluate the learning process.

Feedback is even more critical in the online environment, where students may feel isolated and detached. More than students in traditional settings, online students need appropriate feedback on performance because learning in the online medium is complicated by the disconnection of electronic textual communication. Devoid of the environmental and nonverbal signals available in face-to-face contact, the online classroom requires effective feedback in order to alleviate some of this disconnection and to reduce feelings of isolation in the online student.

Consequently, this chapter will discuss some of the issues facing online faculty members when they try to use feedback to achieve their instructional goals, looking at the two major types of feedback and its various roles. Some actual online student comments will be examined to see what effective feedback is in the online medium. Also, the chapter will present some of the tools available to help online faculty members give constructive feedback to their students and get valuable information back. In particular, midcourse feedback and its applicability to the online classroom will be discussed.

What Is Feedback?

For the purposes of this discussion, a distinction will be made between two types of feedback. *Formative* feedback modifies a student's thinking or behavior for the purpose of learning. *Summative* feedback assesses how well a student accomplishes a task or achieves a result for the purpose of grading.

Formative feedback influences thought and behavior, and can best be seen as motivational. It encourages students to continue down the road they are traveling or to consider changing direction. For example, students need to be encouraged to do the following:

- Stay the course when you are on the right path and have the right idea.
- Modify your thinking or approach when necessary.
- Ask questions.
- Participate.
- Stay on the subject.

Students also need summative feedback. They want to know where they stand in relation to their classmates and, in the case of many adult and online learners, where they stand in relation to their employer's tuition rebate policy. If the student is receiving regular summative feedback, there are few surprises when final grades are given.

The distinction between formative and summative feedback shows how the general role of feedback is to provide a continuous flow of information that helps students to shape the learning process while it is happening and to fulfill their ultimate expectations. The following characteristics should be considered in providing such comprehensive feedback. Feedback should be:

1. *Multidimensional.*   Covers a variety of areas such as content, presentation skills, grammar and other communication techniques.

Note: Material on pages 168 through 169 and 169 through 172 was derived from a summary of a University of Phoenix, 1996 Online Faculty Workshop on Evaluation and Feedback. Used with permission.

2. *Nonevaluative.* Provides objective information about the student's work; allows the student to step back from his or her work and personally acknowledge strengths and weaknesses.
3. *Supportive.* Seeks to offer information in a way that will allow the student to recognize areas for improvement.
4. *Student controlled.* Gives the student choices about how they respond to the information.
5. *Timely.* Best given to the students as soon as possible after completing the assignment or activity.
6. *Specific.* Describes specific observations and makes specific recommendations for the student's consideration.

Effective Online Feedback

Now that we have briefly examined the general nature and characteristics of effective feedback, we can explore how online students judge the quality and quantity of feedback they receive in actual online classes. The following excerpts were taken from University of Phoenix Online Campus student end-of-course surveys. Online students who participated in a variety of undergraduate and graduate business degree programs submitted these end-of-course surveys. The comments were drawn from surveys given during the 1996/97 academic years. The positive and negative comments are useful to you as an online instructor because they help you identify the categories or elements of effective online feedback:

- Timely and thorough
- Formative and summative
- Constructive, supportive, and substantive
- Specific, objective, and individual
- Consistent

Based on the above categories of effective online feedback, online students expect the following:

Prompt, Timely, and Thorough Online Feedback

- *I liked him. He responded almost immediately to any note sent to him. His grading was fair. His knowledge and experience contributed to my enjoyment of this course greatly.*
- *Responses were almost immediate. Very likable and considerate.*
- *Enjoyed working with him as he answered questions in a timely manner, he was flexible and had a sense of humor.*
- *Feedback on our assignments was very timely and helpful.*
- *He was a great motivation, and he always gave feedback in a timely manner.*
- *She was certainly prompt in giving feedback and has enthusiasm for the course.*

- He put in a lot of time by returning every assignment showing corrections to work. I applaud this effort because it really helps complete the learning process. Feedback is essential, even though it is sometimes more difficult in this format. I was always able to go back and recheck my work. A long round of applause.
- He has been most helpful with clarification, as needed. He always returned phone calls immediately and answered back ONLINE notes with a less than 24-hour turn-around time.
- He consistently gets back to students who upload questions and provides thorough explanations in a timely manner.
- All of the questions that were asked of her were answered so everyone understood.

Ongoing Formative Feedback about Online Group Discussions

- She responded to the group on all of our discussions. She also asked follow-up questions of us that required further thought on the issue.
- She sparked some very interesting group discussions, and must have had to absorb mass quantities of feedback from our group.
- At the end of the course he indicated that we had done well interacting with each other and that he had not needed to draw our comments and discussion out of us. What he is missing is that his interaction with us during the course should be a key part of the learning experience. Tossing discussion topics/articles out is not enough for the faculty in this environment. [Online instructors] need to "chime in" occasionally.
- [Online] faculty member needs to be an active participant in the group discussions; this will enhance the learning experience of the group.
- There was very little interaction with the faculty member. Comments were few and far between. Several times I felt as if I was left hanging and some of my classmates seemed to be left to hangout, judging from online discussion.
- The [online] learning environment deteriorates to a constant complaint session when each student takes turn complaining about the inability to understand what the point of specific text data meant. [Instructor] stood by and rarely even acknowledged these complaints and NEVER attempted to clarify any info. The only constructive info provided was AFTER each case was done, he would provide a comprehensive answer of his own.
- Interaction was minimal and only if student initiated. Material uploaded, including the final exam, was the same as in his prior class, per former student. I am not taking a class at Jack in the Box. While a great deal of the material is the same from class to class, the lack of interaction shows a lack of consideration for the learning of students. His approach to what was quality in responses was vague and lacked any detail.
- Altogether, one of the most interactive, supportive, and watchful of the instructors with whom I've studied. He greatly aided my learning.

Ongoing Summative Feedback about Grades

- He was very good at giving us a status of our grades each week. I also appreciated him returning the quiz answers so that it promoted learning.

- *The "student status report" used by this [online] teacher on a daily basis should be required in EVERY course. We never had any doubt about grades.*
- *[We knew] what was in, how we were doing, where the rest of the class was in terms of assignments. When you are a little behind, it is good to know you aren't the only one; conversely, if others have completed assigned work, you know it can be done.*
- *I would have liked more feedback on my performance in each week's assignments. The only measure of performance received was the mid-term.*
- *We got only the most subjective of feedback on any of our work. No grades at all. As a result, I have no real way of anticipating my grade for this class.*
- *Also, I would have liked some feedback on my assignments, and to know how I was going to be graded.*

Constructive, Supportive, and Substantive Online Feedback

- *He is always positive and very constructive with his advice. He keeps the class on track and focused. He uses memos very effectively maintaining a positive tone.*
- *He also offers reassurance that "we'll make it through this research—together."*
- *This faculty member is a wonderful instructor who knows how to reinforce students when they need it. She encourages one to do better and when she offers input, it is always relevant and constructive. She is terrific!*
- *Very pleasant to work with. All comments on submitted work were positive and constructive. I would have preferred to have negative criticisms too. He continually gave us pointers on how not to get stressed out when we were having difficulties with homework or theories. This was very helpful!!!*
- *His instructions were very clear and evaluations and comments accurate and justified. He also helped bring out the importance of others' comments I would not have otherwise realized.*
- *He tried to be motivating in his writings, but on substance, he was thin. Exclamation marks at the end of sentences don't motivate adult learners (!).*
- *His answers were rarely helpful. They usually were cryptic or "cute" leaving me more frustrated and in the dark before I had asked the question.*
- *The [online] faculty member refused to answer any questions just as he did in the first course. When students had problems, his responses were sarcastic, and referenced them back to the problem by saying he thought there was enough information in the problem to answer the question.*
- *I would have liked more "how am I doing?" feedback. His advice was unless you hear otherwise assume your working at an "A" pace....Comments about homework are only 1 or 2 sentences long. She does not tell me topics/points that I have missed so I can better do the next homework.*
- *Excellent instructor! His questions and comments made me think more and gave me thoughts for application now and in the future.*

Specific, Objective, and Individual Online Feedback

- *Specific feedback during the course would be helpful. All we received were subjective comments.*

- *Feedback on individual assignments was extremely instructive.*
- *He set a formidable task for himself in fully grading and commenting on each assignment to each individual. His input and individual attention were very valuable to me.*
- *If he did not take the time to work with me I would have dropped out of the program. Math was very difficult for me and statistics required a lot of math especially learning the formulas.*
- *He was very helpful in answering many of my personal questions that I was quite concerned about. He answered all of these to my satisfaction.*
- *Some feedback on [individual] papers submitted would have been useful.*
- *Did not provide feedback during class on individual performance. I was never sure exactly what I was being graded on—was it just sending in the assignments, my actual words, participation?*
- *There were no clear standards, and I felt my performance was subject to the instructor's beliefs, not my mastery of the material.*

Consistent Online Feedback

- *She gets critical on typographical errors while she herself makes spelling errors.*
- *Demanded too much discipline on turning in homework yet weekly grades were not sent to students in a promised, timely manner. In other words, it's OK to deduct our points for tardiness but there is no compensation for grades and comments to be returned to students in a delayed fashion.*

Giving Online Students Constructive Feedback

The basis of any online feedback is supportive communication. In a famous essay, Jack Gibb described the characteristics of supportive communication and of its opposite, defensive-arousing communication, and thereby as well established the underlying principles of constructive online feedback. Gibb (1961) concluded that communication creates feelings of discomfort and defensiveness when either its content, or the way in which it is presented, makes people feel that they are being:

- Judged
- Manipulated or controlled inappropriately
- Subjected to cold, impersonal treatment
- Treated as a relatively interchangeable person

Gibb recognized that feedback could either support or attack a person's sense of worth and security. The difference between defense-arousing and supportive communication is how the messages are communicated.

Gibb's observations and the preceding online student comments can be combined to determine other "best practices" in the online classroom.

Both sources suggest that online instructors need to practice specific skills when giving constructive feedback to students.

Online feedback should:

1. *Focus on specific behavior rather than on the online student.*   It is important that online instructors refer to what a student *does* rather than to what they think he or she *is*. They might say that an online student "participated too much in a class meeting" rather than that he or she is "dominating." To be told that one is dominating will probably not be as useful as to be told that "in the discussion that just took place, you did not appear to understand what the other students were communicating, and they seemed to have felt forced to accept your arguments." The former approach implies a fixed personality trait; the latter one allows for the possibility of change.

Like everyone else, it is easier for online students to change specific behaviors rather than personalities. Describing one's reactions to behavior allows students to judge the behavior for themselves and to decide how to use it or not use it. The goal is to focus on specific observations, not on inferences. In addition, by avoiding psychological language or speculating on motives, online instructors reduce the need for students to respond defensively (or flame). It encourages online students to make sense of their own behavior.

Focusing on specific behaviors also allows online instructors to share information rather than give advice. By sharing information, an online instructor gives the student responsibility for helping to decide if the feedback is appropriate and in accordance with important goals and needs of the online classroom. When instructors give advice, they can take away important degrees of freedom and discourage taking responsibility. Sharing information puts the focus on developing alternatives, not merely on accepting solutions.

2. *Take the needs of the online student into account.*   Feedback is counterproductive when it serves only instructional needs and fails to consider the needs of the student on the other end of the computer. Constructive feedback is given to help—not because it makes faculty feel better or gives them a psychological advantage. It should also focus on the kind and amount of information the online student can assimilate and use.

3. *Direct your feedback toward behavior the online student can change.* Frustration and aggressive resistance are only increased when an online student is reminded of some shortcoming over which he or she has no control. Attribution theory states that the willingness to change depends on a person's ability to see his or her own efforts contribute to success. Success must be perceived as caused, at least in a substantial part, by one's own efforts.

As teachers, we know that students who believe their efforts influence their achievement are more likely to learn than are students who believe that learning depends on teachers or something else beyond their own control. It works the same for online students.

4. *Help online students to "own" the feedback.*   Constructive feedback is most useful when it is given in the kind of communication climate that encourages the student to actively seek feedback. Constructive online feedback encourages students to be responsible for identifying their strengths and weaknesses and ways of enhancing online performance. One student may concentrate on participating in online discussions more effectively while another may look at how to improve essays. Constructive feedback is often solicited as well as offered.

5. *Give timely online feedback.*   Constructive feedback is most useful immediately after the observed behavior. The online student more readily understands how the information relates to his or her intentions, and thus is in a position to be more accepting of alternative patterns of behavior for trying to solve problems. To the degree that there is a delay in the communication of significant information, there is forgetting, and often what is forgotten is a particular factor that would promote the necessary change in behavior.

6. *Check your online feedback for clarity.*   Having the online student respond to feedback gives you, the instructor, an opportunity to check the accuracy of your feedback.

7. *Consider your online feedback as part of an ongoing relationship.* Constructive feedback opens the way to a relationship with an online student built on communication, growth, and concern. Through such learning relationships, everyone becomes senders and receivers of valuable feedback and experiences.

Using Midcourse Feedback to Improve Online Teaching and Learning

In addition to giving constructive feedback, online instructors need to appreciate and use various sources of information to improve online teaching and learning. While online administrators evaluate course loads, enrollment factors, and other long-range considerations, the online instructor can best explain the reasons for instructional decisions. Online faculty peers can appraise instructional objectives and the currency of subject matter, but it is really online students who are in a better position to comment on classroom teaching skills, course difficulty, and online instructor-student interaction.

Consequently, the clearest picture of an online teaching situation emerges when various perspectives are solicited. In order for online teaching to be effective, it needs to include the feedback of student opinions. A lack of such feedback significantly affects the ability of online faculty to make their instructions and assignments clear and meaningful and open to productive student interpretations. In addition, online teaching and learning are about relationships. A lack of online student feedback significantly affects the quality of the teacher-student communication, making it much more difficult to coordinate meaning.

When interested in online student perceptions, a good place to start is midcourse feedback. Online midcourse feedback takes place about halfway through the online course and involves *structured* questions that ask online students in a given course to describe what helps them learn and how improvements can be made. Pioneered for traditional onsite courses at the University of Washington by D. Joseph Clark (Clark & Bekey, 1979) as a means of evaluating teaching effectiveness, online education can be greatly enhanced by the use of midcourse feedback. Online midcourse feedback can be the basis of a productive course by promoting student-teacher communication. It can become an integral part of the online course.

The Online Midcourse Feedback Procedure

At the beginning of an online course, we introduce the idea of midcourse feedback in the syllabus. The procedure begins with a call for a student volunteer in the syllabus section that outlines the third week of the five- or six-week course (the fifth week of a traditional 10-week course). The syllabus informs the online students that they should send a message to one of their classmate's personal mailbox (a volunteer to be determined later) where they will list: (1) three areas that are working well in this course and (2) three ways to improve the class. The volunteer will then combine all of the messages—verbatim and unedited—and send them to the instructor.

We ask that no names be attached to this information so that all participants remain anonymous. Of course, we are not able to distinguish the volunteer's comments from others. We explain how the information will be used to make changes for the last two weeks of the course and for future courses. We conclude with comments about how much we appreciate their honesty and participation. We also point out that the students will receive a formal end-of-the-course evaluation form from the university administration. We encourage them to wait until after they have completed the midcourse feedback and have received our responses before they send in the official student evaluation to the administration. The midcourse feedback usually responds to many online student questions and concerns.

At any rate, it is important for online students to understand what the process can and cannot do and how it differs from the formal end-of-the-course student evaluations. The process is voluntary, anonymous, and confidential for the online students. Students are not required to respond; if they do, they will remain anonymous; and only the online instructor will see the information—it is not intended for administrators. Because midcourse feedback is not a formal evaluation, it encourages a safe environment for online student feedback.

The strength of information from online midcourse feedback for students is that it can be used to change things immediately, even in a five-week course. For example, in one online midcourse feedback procedure, students in a Managerial Ethics and Responsibility course responded that they would prefer to locate related articles from the Internet rather than read assigned articles (that were slightly outdated) from the text. The instructor was able to respond by allowing the students to locate Internet articles for the last two weeks of class. This particular information resulted in positive comments in the formal end-of-the-course evaluations and in a number of good articles that the online instructor was later able to use in other classes.

After introducing and describing the procedure in the syllabus, we upload a reminder message in the third week of class and ask for a volunteer. Typically, two or three students respond either in the main meeting room or through the instructor's personal mailbox. We then send the following message to the main meeting for everyone to read:

```
To:       MbXXX Mgt592
From:     [Your name]
Subject:  Midcourse Feedback
Written:  Tues Feb 17 at 9:04AM
```

Thanks for volunteering, Joe. I usually do this "first come, first serve," so if it's OK with the rest of the class, you're it.

Everyone else will send you his or her comments by this Wednesday. These comments should include 2–3 ideas about what's working well in this class, and 2–3 areas that need improvement. Like in all constructive feedback, the positive comments should come first.

Remember not to send suggestions to the open forum where names can be associated with specific comments.

Please compile the feedback verbatim under the two categories— WHAT'S WORKING WELL, and AREAS FOR IMPROVEMENT (in that order)—and don't do any editing. The compilation should be done anonymously with no names attached to any information.

Then send the compilation to my personal mailbox. I'll add my responses and send all the information back to the open forum verbatim for all students to read.

Thanks again, Joe, for volunteering and to everyone for participating. I appreciate it.

The online students then send their responses to the following two questions to the student volunteer's (Joe's) personal mailbox:

1. What helps you learn in this course?
2. What improvements would you like, and how would you suggest they be made?

After the online students send their comments to the volunteer, the task is to compile the comments verbatim and without any editing. Seeking themes is an important part of midcourse feedback, but it is also important to look for differences and areas of disagreement. Online students always see the course and instructor from differing perspectives. Some say the reading load for the course is too great, while others counter that this is not the case. These kinds of comparisons are useful for both the online students and the instructor because they contextualize individual student perceptions and insights about the course and test them in a public forum. If everyone does not share a statement, the instructor and the student who made the comment can better judge the statement's significance. Consequently, the compilation never summarizes the information but presents it as "raw data" in order to maintain the integrity of individual statements.

A typical example of a midcourse feedback compilation looks like the following:

To: [Your name]
From: Joe Smith
Subject: Midcourse Assessment
Written: Thurs Feb 19 at 7:45pm

Here's the compilation of the comments I received from the other students in the class.

WHAT'S WORKING WELL:

1. I think the course content is excellent. There is a good mix of the text material and lecture information. The added feature of classmate input really rounds out the material. Using a problem from your current work area is a nice touch.

2. I was a little skeptical of this online format because of the indirect interaction. I have been totally pleased with the outcome. I think the interaction has been excellent and very beneficial.

3. I feel that the class syllabus was well laid out and was very easy to follow. I knew exactly what was expected of myself and on what day it was expected.

4. The instructor had some good assignments that helped me to understand the point he was trying to convey to us. Also the points of the other classmates helped to broaden my outlook on issues.

5. We used our own work place to apply to our assignments which pointed out many improvements that could be made and it showed me why certain problems existed.

6. The class discussions are great! The opportunity to converse with one another on each lecture is a learning experience indeed.

7. I like the exercises too. These provide a chance for us to learn about ourselves.

8. I like the fact that I can sit here in front of my computer, dressed any way I please, at any hour of the day I please, and "attend" class.

9. I really liked the additional information the instructor provided outside the lectures.

10. The consistency of the assignment schedule each week. This helps because we are all working individuals and we can schedule around the weekly class schedule.

11. The response part of the assignment. When we respond it ensures that we read each other's views on the question and that we compare each other's views.

12. The chapters that are combined each week seem to compliment each other and flow well with the syllabus and work retrospectively as the weeks go by.

AREAS FOR IMPROVEMENT:

1. Group discussions that require consensus. I don't believe that we can do this effectively with the random way we individually handle our online sessions.
2. Whether needed or not the class should be aware of the online etiquette at the very beginning of class. This could be supported through an assignment.
3. The use of the first syllabus as a guide and then not reiterating this in the following weeks. I was and still am having to go back and forth between the initial syllabus and comparing it to the assignments. Although this may be an organizational problem of mine.
4. I would have liked to have seen an example of a well-written short report.
5. Personally, I need to organize my time more efficiently in order to balance the demands of my family, my full-time job, my part-time job, and this course.
6. When we need feedback from instructor, please follow through with it.
7. If people cannot send in assignments due to various situations, please have them contact the instructor to inform other classmates. Our feedback sometimes relies on individual input and we wonder why we haven't heard anything. It holds up the other students at times.
8. The only thing I can think of that hasn't gone well was the exercise to reach a layoff consensus. The exercise was interesting, but I think the online interaction system was stretched just a little too far. The communication sequence was tough to maintain and sometimes the timing of answers was out of sync.

It is then important to respond to students' feedback as soon as possible. A sample of the kinds of responses we send back to online students follows:

```
To:       MbXXX MGT592
From:     [Your name]
Subject:  Midcourse Feedback Responses
Written:  Fri Feb 20 at 8:10am
```

Below are responses to your course comments. I follow specific comments with my responses enclosed in ***asterisks***.

3. The use of the first syllabus as a guide and then not reiterating this in the following weeks. I was and still am having to go back and forth between

the initial syllabus and comparing it to the assignments. Although this may be an organizational problem of mine.

No, I see your point. What I can begin to do is reiterate the relevant parts of the syllabus at the beginning of each week's lecture. Thanks.

4. I would have liked to see an example of a well-written short report.

You're right! I will send an example of an excellent short report to the "MbXXX Reports" branch meeting right away.

5. Personally, I need to organize my time more efficiently in order to balance the demands of my family, my full-time job, my part-time job, and this course.

Don't we all! Online classes are a commitment.

6. When we need feedback from instructor, please follow through with it.

I'm assuming that I do. Would someone give me a more specific example?

7. If people cannot send in assignments due to various situations, please have them contact the instructor to inform other classmates. Our feedback sometimes relies on the individual input and we wonder why we haven't heard anything. It holds up the other students at times.

I do send personal messages to students who have not sent their work in, but it's a good idea to suggest that they also inform the class. I need to encourage more personal responsibility in this area.

8. The only thing I can think of that hasn't gone well was the exercise to reach a layoff consensus. The exercise was interesting, but I think the online interaction system was stretched just a little too far. The communication sequence was tough to maintain and sometimes the timing of answers was out of sync.

Reaching consensus online is particularly challenging. But I think you did a very good job. In addition, it's not so much that you reach a perfect consensus, but that you learn something on the way. But I'll keep your point in mind. Maybe I can do a better job of summarizing the level of consensus along the way. Thanks.

Benefits and Limitations of the Midcourse Feedback

Like other sources of information, midcourse feedback offers benefits and limitations. Based on online student comments, midcourse feedback is successful and associated with several advantages: The process builds on a positive foundation of what works well, it offers different categories than standardized ratings, its midcourse timing allows instructors to make changes during the same class, and its feedback contains specific suggestions on how to make those changes.

Midcourse feedback is especially useful in online classrooms because it is more personal than individual student ratings and allows students to read what other students are thinking. Its group orientation builds on existing associations and reinforces the online learner's expectations for sharing experiences and for developing social cohesion. Basically, midcourse feedback emphasizes that online students have a role in shaping their own instruction and learning.

On the other hand, midcourse feedback has its limits. If used as a summative procedure for hiring or firing online faculty, the process can stifle open communication with students, not to mention creating extraordinary faculty anxiety and distrust of the process. Students usually share honest information and constructive perspectives about their courses because it is designed to help faculty improve their teaching. When midcourse information is used otherwise, students can become reluctant to share opinions they feel threaten their instructors. Consequently, maintaining midcourse feedback as a formative process—voluntary, anonymous and confidential—helps to encourage open communication and meaningful online student feedback.

Mentoring New Online Faculty with the Midcourse Feedback

We also use midcourse feedback to help mentor beginning online faculty. It is particularly useful in a mentoring process. New online instructors often need to learn about specific aspects of their initial teaching. One major advantage of midcourse feedback is that the questions can be tailored to respond to the concrete needs of online instructors. For example, a recently mentored online instructor wanted to know if his students were gaining a thorough understanding of the dynamics between theory and business practice in class discussions. Another beginning online instructor wanted information on course structure and the incorporation of current news items into the curriculum. In both of these situations, we worked with the instructors to frame specific midcourse feedback questions that would get directly at their concerns. The flexibility of the midcourse feedback procedure offered opportunities to respond to the mentored instructors' concerns by changing generic questions in order to address more immediate needs.

Soon after the midcourse feedback, we telephone the mentored instructor and discuss the information, answering questions, explaining comments, and offering alternative interpretations of apparent contradictions. During this phase, the task is to acknowledge online student perspectives. The intent is not to persuade the new online faculty member to agree with the students; rather, it is to highlight themes and explanations that integrate student and instructor perceptions.

Occasionally, online students flame an instructor and write negative comments in a harsh way. In these cases, we emphasize that student comments are only one perspective. We try to encourage a cooperative venture in problem solving with the mentored online instructor by sharing our own relevant teaching experiences and suggesting where online students may be "coming from." In this manner, we try to promote reflection on the issues, not just on the students' words. The conversation can then move to strategies for constructive change.

Conclusion

Just as there is no simple system for evaluating the quality of online learning, there is no simple system for evaluating the quality of online teaching. However, by thinking carefully about the purposes of feedback, and by crafting multiple methods of giving and getting online feedback, one can devise effective and constructive approaches. The process of thinking about online feedback focuses attention on the practice of good online teaching and helps create another educational culture in which teaching and learning are highly valued.

Online feedback can make a positive contribution to online instructional improvement and student learning. As a formative, summative, and supportive process for online teaching and learning, constructive feedback can be a trusted form of instructor and student information. It can be a catalyst for change in a variety of online teaching and learning settings.

References

Chickering, A. W., & Gamson, Z. F. (1987). *Seven Principles for Good Practice in Undergraduate Education: Faculty Inventory.* Racine, WI: The Johnson Foundation, Inc.

Clark, D. J., & Bekey, J. (1979). Use of small groups in instructional evaluation. *POD Quarterly, 1* (2), 87–95.

Gibb, J. (1961). Defensive communication. *Journal of Communication, 11,* 134–148.

EPILOGUE: THE HUMAN PROMISE

BOB WEIGHT AND TERRI BISHOP

When Ken White asked us to write an epilogue to this book and to offer a brief retrospective on what it was like to pioneer the development of an online campus, our first response was, "We've only just begun!" Both of us were with the University of Phoenix (UOP) Online Campus from the beginning—Terri as its first director and Bob as its first instructor. We both have experienced incredible change in the field. In a world that did not exist 10 years ago, today's colleges and universities across the country are plunging headlong into online education. But even as universities are spurred by competition for students and stampede onto the online scene, we see the need to address fundamental questions: What is the promise of technology and education? What is the reality of the social change it represents? What are the continuing challenges?

When UOP conceived and developed the Online Campus in 1989, it was halfway between being a small struggling campus of eight students in 1976 and being the nation's largest private university it is today. The University's programs now serve working adult students from throughout the world. On the average, these adult students have worked in a career-oriented position for 11 years and about 80 percent of them study business or management, while others study nursing, education, counseling, or information systems.

The Online Campus was created as an extension of UOP's essential mission. Its purpose is to provide educational services to working adult students whose access to higher education is either restricted or nonexistent. A pioneer in the field, the Online Campus has effectively served this purpose and has exceeded most predictions for survival. Financial success, student and employer satisfaction, and academic accountability systems have brought an attendant degree of respect. Despite its for-profit status—loved by the financial community and scorned by academic traditionalists—university and college administrators and others vested in higher education are now looking carefully at what we are doing. The realities of financially ailing colleges and universities and the overarching reach of educational technology have created an environment ready to embrace change.

Today, online education and other forms of communications technology are creating a national and international market for higher education. Cooperative initiatives such as the Western Governors University and the California Virtual University are helping to globalize the higher education marketplace. Corporate universities, training organizations, and publishers are also emerging to compete for students.

Although this confluence of events and rapid change offers little time for reflection, it is crucial that such reflection takes place. We appreciate that organizations such as the Western Interstate Commission for Higher Education and the American Council on Education have emerged to provide standards and guidelines for quality distance learning. Without such reflection, we cannot design the principles of good practice that better serve our future. Now, more than ever, we need to consider what online education really offers students.

Online Education and the Technological Promise

Our initial observation is that many of the champions of online education make a technological promise to learners. The *virtual campus* and the *classroom without walls* are common metaphors for the new technology's ability to convey information through text, graphics, voice, and video to anyone on the global network. The discussion commonly revolves around hardware purchases, the best applications, the cost of using the Internet, or how to get faculty to adopt more technology.

This promise is often depicted as an alternative to increased human effort, and its attraction centers on its comparative effectiveness. The argument is nothing new. Radio, television, satellite and cable transmission, and videocassettes have all been promoted as promising better ways of delivering education. Although the promise has sometimes been fulfilled and at other times has not, technology continues to move at unfathomable speeds, ever challenging higher education to keep up.

We understand the attraction of technology—it has been with us since the infancy of UOP's Online Campus. In the early days, when online bulletin boards were in their heyday, we were excited about the capabilities of 400-baud modems and about how 1,200-baud modems were becoming available. We experimented with various communications software programs. Microsoft was only beginning to make an entry onto desktops and there was no World Wide Web. Everything had to be accomplished manually—from setting up the modem, logging on to the server, to selecting the mailboxes from which one wanted to read messages. Many early online faculty members loved to build script files to automate technological processes, challenged by the fact that the technology of online communication was cumbersome at best. It was an exciting time.

On the other hand, and retrospectively, we now see that the essence of technology could always be reduced to its most fundamental and powerful element—that is, electronically facilitated human dialogue. Consequently, we needed to question whether online education is a story about technology or a story about social change during a technological age.

At the beginning of the Online Campus, it was commonplace in many traditional educational institutions to teach 200 students face to face in lecture-hall fashion. Nevertheless, many critics of online education argued that face-to-face instruction was the only way to have an impact on student learning. In contrast, we encouraged UOP online instructors to become the facilitators, guides, and even co-learners in their small class groups, rather than the sole source of all knowledge. We now see that our success was founded on how well online faculty members were able to adapt the technology in order to connect with students and to create meaning from the human—rather than the technological—connection. Instead of depending on the technological promise alone, we used the technology as a tool to enable human relationships to form and interactive learning to occur. We decided to depend on the human promise.

Online Education and the Human Promise

Both of us agree that the major lesson we have learned from our experiences is that the key to success in online education is the attitude of online faculty members. The faculty have to disabuse themselves of the idea that they are the sole experts in electronic classroom and that students are "sitting at their feet," waiting to hear pearls of wisdom issue forth. Instructors have a great deal of knowledge and experience to share with students. But it is the way in which this is done that makes all the difference in the electronic medium.

The Online Campus is about using technology to build human community and that is in no small part accomplished by the talent and enthusiasm of faculty members like those represented in this book. Ours is not a traditional faculty. They are a faculty of working professionals with real-world experience in their fields of expertise. They are CPAs, attorneys, chief information officers, general managers, human resource professionals, and engineers—all who sign up to teach what they practice during working hours.

Unlike traditional faculty, online instructors are even more challenged by the need for a human attitude—the human promise of online education. Technology naturally lends itself to one-way and stark communication. It is easy for faculty (and some students) to pontificate at great length. The online medium is fundamentally sterile and lacks normal communications clues. But online learning requires human commitment to take place, and that means dialogue similar to what most people experienced in senior seminar classes in college. In other words, online faculty members have to facilitate a communication environment where an informal style is encouraged, where questions are welcomed, and where haughtiness and arrogance are discouraged.

Consequently, online faculty members have to be motivated by a set of assumptions different from the more traditional educational models. Under the UOP approach to education, online students perform many important roles and, in general, assume more responsibility for learning than under more traditional "teacher-directed models."

First, online faculty members must assume that students are motivated to learn; otherwise, they would not be here. Therefore, although we may use traditional measures of evaluation like quizzes and tests, we do not "check up" on students. It is our intention to treat students as fellow business professionals who want to learn new skills and concepts and will do what is suggested to accomplish that goal.

Second, online faculty members must assume that students are accomplished adults who have achieved some level of success in their business careers and who already know a great deal about management and business. Therefore, students are considered a learning resource, the same as the textbook and instructor. Almost all students have valuable experiences from which they can learn. It is important for them to share their experiences with their fellow students and apply their experiences to topics of discussion.

In other words, online students and faculty members are often on a peer level. The online faculty member becomes a mentor and facilitator rather than an expert or authority. Consequently, online instructors establish informal and supportive learning environments under which disagreement and dissenting views are encouraged.

Third, the online instructor must assume a level of involvement quite different from a traditional one. Even though most online faculty members have full-time jobs outside of teaching, they need to be available to students by phone and through electronic mail at reasonable times. Clearly, the most important aspect in online success is to be continuously visible. This means logging on on a daily basis and sometimes even twice a day. It also means that online faculty share aspects of their lives so that they come across as real people and not just sterile words on a computer screen. Talking about their "real jobs," about their children, and their leisure activities adds to the richness of the online world and humanizes its sterility.

Perhaps the importance of the human promise to online education is best illustrated by the story of one of our early online students. "Tom" was a medical doctor practicing in southern California when he decided to seek an MBA. Prompted largely by the shifting sands of the health-care environment, Tom realized that managed care would require managers. Medical school did not prepare Tom for business, and since his focus had changed to that aspect of health care, knowing the rules and understanding the principles of business became imperative. However, achieving this goal without "missing a beat" would be more elusive.

Tom looked at traditional programs, evening programs, and programs designed specifically for physicians. None offered the flexibility he needed for his variable schedule and travel. Then he read about UOP's Online Campus. Tom thought it was an intriguing idea: electronic-mediated learning that was both interactive and able to be accomplished on a busy schedule.

The rest is history. In a two-year period, Tom lugged his little monochrome laptop throughout the country. He studied in airports, traffic jams, at 3:00 A.M., and during boring meetings. He would study in the local laundromat at 4:00 A.M. every morning before his family woke up. He logged on from every imaginable configuration of telephone, and once had the maintenance man at a hotel in Canada look for a hook up by disassembling the main box entering the hotel—service beyond belief. At another time, Tom even had his textbook mailed overnight to Yellowstone National Park when he forgot it one summer.

Through all of this, Tom never did "miss a beat." His family was patient as he woke early on vacation and "went to study." They become familiar with the sound of the modem's mating call as it hissed and squealed. Tom's colleagues viewed the entire process with disbelief. With all Tom had to do, how could he possibly get an MBA in the meantime?

Well, Tom's colleagues know better than anyone else that it can be done. Tom's education has been invaluable. It has given him the tools to understand and evaluate information better, a vital part of business.

Most importantly, though, the pace of the Online Campus was fast and furious, Tom understood that it was the online students and faculty who helped him succeed. Although he never met any of them face to face, he got to know many of them and, without exception, found them to be exceptional people.

At the end of his program, although Tom was really glad to be nearly done, he looked back on the experience as a very personal one. Soon, he retired the old laptop that was dented and scratched and replaced it with a shiny new desktop. He cleared his den of MBA "stuff" and learned how to sleep past 6:00 A.M. But we are convinced that what he will never forget is the online people—the human promise.

Conclusion

Developing the first successful online educational program has been a wild and very satisfying ride. Online is not only a great way to provide education to a widespread clientele but it is also a great way to meet people and to get to know them better. People are constantly amazed when they are told that online faculty get to know their students better than many conventional classroom teachers. Even though people are starting to accept as commonplace stories about people meeting on the Internet, falling in love, and getting married, they still doubt the human potential of the online classroom. But we know differently. Technology makes online education possible, but it is the people that matter. People are the real promise of any learning, including online education. They are the reality of the social and educational change that online teaching and learning represent.

The continuing challenge is to keep people and dialogue at the center of this dynamic and exciting learning medium.

INDEX